WARRIOR WOMEN
ARISE

McDougal & Associates

*Servants of Christ and Stewards of the
Mysteries of God*

WARRIOR WOMEN
ARISE

BY

AMANDA
GORANSSON

Cover Design by Bas van den Eijkhof

Published by:
McDougal & Associates
18896 Greenwell Springs Road
Greenwell Springs, Louisiana 70739
www.thepublishedword.com

McDougal & Associates is an organization dedicated to spreading the Gospel of the Lord Jesus Christ to as many people as possible in the shortest time possible.

ISBN 978-1-934769-31-7

Printed on demand in the US, the UK, Australia and Sweden
For worldwide distribution

DEDICATION

To the members of my women's prayer group:

You are all truly women warriors, and without your love and prayers in the midst of the battle, this book would never have been born.

CONTENTS

The Lord gives the command;
The women who proclaim the good tidings
* are a great host.*

Psalm 68:11, NASB

INTRODUCTION

Are you a woman who has a place inside you which cries out for destiny, a place that few, if any, see, one burning with longing for the extraordinary, where you live out your dreams and where the giftings and callings of God have been implanted before the very beginning of time? Are you someone who hears about the great feats of others from the past and present and longs to be known as one who follows God radically and courageously? Have you felt a stirring deep inside you over the past weeks and months for something more in your walk with God? Perhaps you are someone who had such a longing at one time, but the reality of life has left you exhausted or cynical, and your dreams lie smashed on the rocks of suffering and hardship. Are you so caught up in life's daily worries and demands that you have not even considered that there is something more? If you are any of these women, this book is dedicated to you. It is a cry from the heart of the Father for His daughters to rise up and become all He has always planned for them to be.

Each one of us has a task to accomplish, a place to fill in the last-day army of the living God. The job we have to do has been specifically designed and planned to fit our personalities, giftings, and callings. God is now sending forth a trumpet call for us to rise up and dare to take our place.

Psalm 68:11 speaks prophetically of a *"great host,"* or army, of women being released to proclaim the Word of God. It is time for us, as women, to be unveiled as the mighty warriors we are. We are part of an end-time army destined to bring in the greatest harvest of all time. We are called to change nations, person by person and family by family.

I believe that Father God is blowing upon His girls in this hour, with a gentle, yet powerful wind. He is breathing life into this valley of dry bones, and as He does, an army will arise. As Father God blows, the false perceptions concerning our identity, which we have received from the enemy, the church, and even ourselves, will be removed, and we will stand as His mighty servants.

Women, it is our hour to rise up and become all that God has destined us to be. It is time for an army of women to be released throughout the earth, an army that will not be intent on seeking its own glory but, rather, on preparing the way for the Bridegroom, Jesus.

This will be an army of breathtakingly feminine warriors who will fight side by side with men, a host of women who are ferocious when it comes to opposing the enemy's powers, while at the same time being clothed with the cloak of humility and gentleness toward others. We are destined to be like nothing ever seen before, and now is the time for God's secret weapon to be unleashed.

You may never have thought of yourself as being capable of being a warrior. Perhaps that is even a frightening and threatening concept for you. But deep within you resides a lioness, and she wants out. This book is a war cry directed to the women of God, a cry for them to enter into battle and embrace their destiny, a cry for freedom for God's princesses. Now is your hour, mighty women of God. Will you heed the cry of the Father's heart: *Warrior Women, Arise?*

— Amanda Goransson
Gothenburg, Sweden

Chapter 1

WOMEN WARRIORS UNVEILED

THE YEAR WAS 1429, AND A YOUNG AND UNEDUCATED peasant girl dressed in knight's armor rode on a white horse. She was followed by an army of men whom she was leading into battle, with the purpose of regaining control of a town which was being held under siege by an enemy nation. She held a white banner in her hands, and her words of encouragement to the soldiers resounded in the air: "Courage! Do not fall back: in a little, the place will be yours. Watch! When you see the wind blow my banner against the bulwark, you shall take it! In, in, the place is yours." [1] The soldiers fought all day and received the victory promised them as evening drew to a close.

This young warrior woman was Joan of Arc, and she was instrumental in the first significant victory for the French people at that time. Her actions ultimately changed the course of the nation. But how could an unlearned girl have been used to rally and lead troops into war? Joan of Arc claimed to have received visitations and messages from angelic beings from the time she was just thirteen years old. These messengers proclaimed to her that God Himself was calling her to be His instrument to vindicate her nation and restore their rightful king to the throne.

When Joan reached the age of about seventeen, she felt led by God to approach France's king in hiding. She boldly traveled to him through enemy territory, determined to obey her Lord. She proclaimed: "I do not fear their soldiers; my way lies open. If there are soldiers on the road, I have my Lord with me, who will make a road for me to reach the Dauphin [the rightful king]. I was born for this." [2] Thus, one woman, obeying a calling from her Lord Jesus, defied the political, social, and church structure of the day and changed the course of history in the process.

Joan of Arc dared to believe that an individual could hear words of destiny from God Himself, and in little more than a year's time, she helped to rally troops for war, crown a king, and restore hope to a broken country. The Catholic Church, however, was outraged at her audacity to claim that she could hear from God for herself, and, as a result, she was imprisoned and put on trial for heresy. During her trial, which was, to say the very least, unjust and politically staged, Joan of Arc displayed great courage, wisdom, and boldness in her answers, shattering all preconceived ideas of what an uneducated peasant woman was capable of.

Joan was ultimately condemned to be burned at the stake for heresy, and her final recorded words were these: "I pray you, go to the nearest church, and bring me the cross, and hold it up level with my eyes until I am dead. I would have the cross on which God hung be ever before my eyes while life lasts in me." [3] Then, as she was dying in the flames, she was said to have called out, "Jesus. Jesus!" [4]

Joan of Arc lived between 1412 and 1431, nearly six hundred years ago now, and yet her legacy continues to intrigue and inspire us today. She is one of the many women whom God chose through the course of history to impact nations. Although she never killed anyone herself and often wept at the sight of the bloodshed of war, she did lead physical armies into battle. I do not believe that our Lord is calling us into a physical battle today, but the life of this godly woman can inspire and empower us in this hour. Her testimony demolishes the argument that God cannot use women in warfare.

When interrogated about her decision to leave her village and embrace her destiny, Joan said, "It pleased God thus to act through a simple maid in order to turn back the king's enemies." [5] I believe these words ring true as a prophetic statement for the warrior women God is calling today. Does it not again please our God to use simple women, women like you and me, to turn back His enemies?

The circumstances in which we find ourselves today bear much similarity to the state of France in the time of Joan of Arc. It was a torn and divided nation. A king was on the throne who was not the legal heir, half the nation was in league with the enemy (England), and those who supported the true heir to the throne were weak and afraid to act. Enemy forces had sown fear and intimidation into French society, paralyzing those who possessed true authority. It was in this hopeless state that

God raised up His champion of the hour, a young girl of no influence or importance, whose only weapon was her obedience to the voice of her heavenly King, Jesus.

How very like the situation in which we find ourselves today! Our world is under the power of an enemy king (Satan) who has established himself as lord over the nations through deception and theft. This king seeks to influence people in many high positions of society in order to control the minds and thought patterns of whole nations.

At the same time, the church, made up of those who are true to the rightful King, Jesus, remains in fear and unbelief, not daring to oppose this usurper of the throne. It is for this reason that our Lord needs obedient and willing messengers who will arise, proclaiming the truth of the Gospel, and restoring hope and courage to the soldiers of God's army, causing them to stand up and fight and proclaim the King of all Kings as the rightful Ruler of the nations of this world. Could it not be that you and I are called to be part of the answer that is so desperately needed?

As we noted earlier, Psalm 68:11-12 speaks prophetically of an army of women being released to proclaim the Word, or message, of God and bring defeat to the camp of the enemy:

The Lord gives the command;
The women who proclaim the good tidings are a great
    host:

"Kings of armies flee, they flee,
And she who remains at home will divide the spoil!"

NASB

This *"great host,"* or army, will speak with such authority that even enemy kings will be turned away in fear.

Some Bible translations have failed to record that it is a host of *"women"* who will proclaim these good tidings, despite the fact that the Hebrew verb used here carries a feminine form, rather than the more common masculine. This may be because the idea of an army of women is, and long has been, a very foreign concept to most. The army of women being released under the directive of their God will definitely have the benefit of an element of surprise. Who would have thought that God would use women to defeat His enemies?

Ed Silvoso discussed this phenomenon in his book *Women, God's Secret Weapon*. He wrote: "The Scriptures tell us that the day is fast approaching when God will lift women up and release masses of them into ministry. Psalm 68:11 declares that at a strategic time God will give a command, and a company of women who proclaim the good news will defeat His enemies. An all-female army will bring this about, and it will be a surprise victory." [6]

Cindy Jacobs also discussed this idea in her book *Women of Destiny*. She wrote, in her commentary on these verses, "Psalm 68:11 is a prophetic message for the great army of women who are arising in the land. 'The Lord gives the word of power: the women who bear *and* pub-

17

lish [the news] are a great host' (AMP). According to Dr. Gary Greig, this passage and Isaiah 40:9-10 both refer to God raising up an army of women evangelists in the last days, since both refer to the Lord appearing in glory to bring judgment on the earth and to restore His people in the land of Israel. The verb forms in both passages are in the feminine, and not the usual masculine form of the verbs in question." [7]

God has something planned that we have never seen before, and the army He is raising up will walk in such power that *"kings and armies flee in haste."* Even the housewives remaining at home will receive plunder from this war. Those of us who may not be able to engage in the frontline battle will still receive a reward. I believe that in the days ahead, as God not only calls, but also empowers us as warriors, we will be able to say, with Joan of Arc, "I was born for this."

We must not believe that this will occur through our own power or capabilities. Joan of Arc was often seen praying and weeping before God, asking for His help to accomplish that which she was called to do. In the same way, we will be constantly dependent upon God's power and not our own. It may very well be in our moments of greatest anguish that the power of God will be unleashed from within us.

Even the great apostle Paul struggled with this issue of human weakness. He had a thorn in his side, and it taunted him and caused him great pain. On three different occasions he asked the Lord to remove it, but the answer he received was this: *"My grace is suf-*

ficient for you, for my power is made perfect in weakness" (2 Corinthians 12:9). You may feel that there are areas in your life that cause you great grief, and are a source of weakness, yet these need not hinder you in your calling as a warrior. Surrendered to the Lord, these may be the very weapons which will be used to crush the head of the enemy.

The whole concept of a woman warrior may be totally foreign to you, as it is to many. *Warrior* is not the stereotypical description we usually hear regarding the female gender. Instead, we are often associated with characteristics such as gentleness, compassion, nurturing, and love. Nevertheless, God is challenging us to discover that there is so much more to us, as His girls. We are made in His image, and one of the names He calls Himself is Lord of Hosts, which means that He's the leader of a great army. Our God is a warrior and, as His daughters, so are we.

Moses and Miriam described God in this way:

> *"The LORD is a warrior;*
> *the LORD is his name."*   Exodus 15:3

This was after God had defeated the Egyptian army, one of the most powerful armies of the time. And the Old Testament is filled with other examples of God leading His people into battle against their enemies so that they could receive their proper inheritance. Because He was a warrior, so were they.

The description the Bible gives of the way in which Jesus will return to this earth should leave no doubt in our minds that we follow a fierce and determined warrior God:

> *I saw heaven standing open and there before me was a white horse, whose rider is called Faithful and True. With justice he judges and makes war. His eyes are like blazing fire, and on his head are many crowns. He has a name written on him that no one knows but he himself. He is dressed in a robe dipped in blood, and his name is the Word of God. The armies of heaven were following him, riding on white horses and dressed in fine linen, white and clean. Out of his mouth comes a sharp sword with which to strike down the nations.*
>
> Revelation 19:11-15

This is a far cry from the vulnerable baby Jesus came as, when He first made His appearance on earth. I believe God is wanting us to identify with Him, not only as a lamb, but also as a lion, to whom all authority in heaven and on earth has been given.

The clearest example we have in Scripture of a warrior woman is Deborah. She was a judge over the Israelites and also a prophetess, and yet she was a woman just like us. She had feelings, needs, and fears, but most of all she had a destiny. She arose in Israel as a mother at a time when few were willing or had the strength to fight. Understanding the times, she saw the needs among God's people and arose to face them—not in her own strength, but in the power of her God.

When we read Deborah's song, sung after a great victory over enemy troops, we are given an insight into the attitudes of her heart. This woman did not glory in her own successes but revealed an attitude of honor and support for the princes of God, stating:

"My heart is with Israel's princes,
  with the willing volunteers among the people."

Judges 5:9

In her song, Deborah addressed the need for action in regard to the situation that existed at that time. Her position as a warrior was simply a response to that need. In the very same way, this spirit of willingness and desire for the good of God's people will permeate the warrior women who will now begin to arise.

We will not rise up in order to seek glory for ourselves or to denounce the role of men in God's army. Instead, we will take our place beside His princes, so that together with them we can fight against the enemies of our God and see victory.

We were never meant to fight alone. The name *Barak* (the commander of Israel's army in Deborah's time) and also the name of Deborah's husband (*Lappidoth*) meant "light" or "the shining one." I believe that as Deborah arose to go into battle, the men around her also shone, as they were meant to.

In the very beginning of time, God called Adam and Eve because together they represented His perfect plan and reflected His image. Man is not complete without the woman, and woman is not complete without the man. In the last-day battle which is coming, we will rise as a united force, men and women together, working in perfect unity.

Deborah was a prophetess, meaning that she heard from God and was then able to communicate His heart and wisdom to His people. The Bible states that the people of Israel came to Deborah to have their disputes settled, for God had endowed her with wisdom, discernment, and the ability to resolve conflict. She thus worked to bring peace and justice among her own people, but she was also not afraid to go out to war against God's enemies.

In the recorded history of the judges, known by that very name, it seems apparent that Deborah had never planned to go out to the battle herself. She had simply given the word of the Lord to Barak, the commander of the army, but Barak asked her to accompany him and his troops to war, as he did not want to fight alone.

It has been said by some that Barak was worn out from years of fighting, and that may or may not have been the case, but whatever the reason, he did invite Deborah to go along, and it proved to be a wise move on his part. How many men in the church today have faithfully stood in their positions, fighting for the welfare of the children of God, and are now battle-weary as a result? In fact, many are exhausted, disillusioned, and on the verge of burnout. They have been faithful and deserve honor, but when only a small portion of the body turns out to fight, is it any wonder that those who do the fighting are weary beyond words?

God Himself has said that it is not good for man to be alone:

The LORD God said, "It is not good for the man to be alone. I will make a helper suitable for him."

Genesis 2:18

The Hebrew word for *helper* in this passage is the same one used when God was to break in and save His people, so our help is real. It is time for warrior women to be released among the armies of God, to strengthen, complement, and encourage our men, so that together we can lead the church of the living God to victory. Just as Deborah was needed in her time, I believe some Deborahs are needed today.

Deborah is described in Scripture not only as a judge and a warrior, but also as a mother in Israel. I believe that these particular qualities are inherent in all women—an ability to discern, a yearning to nurture and bring justice, and a fierce resolution to defend family or other areas of authority or responsibility. Deborah was the lioness of the kingdom, and we need some more lionesses today.

Throughout recorded history, going forth to war and fighting has been considered primarily a man's task, but there have been times (in the absence of qualified men or when a woman's village or family was in imminent danger) when women have taken up the fight. I feel confident that all of us who are mothers will agree: When it comes to our children, no matter what our personality or fears, if they are being attacked in any way, an unrelenting urge to protect them and remove the threat instinctively surfaces in us. For those who don't yet have children, it may be that when an area of your work, marriage, friendships, or calling is being threatened, a fighting spirit suddenly arises within you. God, our Creator, has placed that instinct within each of us.

The name *Deborah* actually means "honeybee." In a real hive of honeybees, there is a queen, and the rest are drones or workers. Interestingly enough, it is only the females who have stingers, and when the hive is attacked or is in danger from any source, these female bees swarm and go on the offensive. Most of the time their tasks are much less dramatic: looking after the young, keeping the hive clean, and, when they are older, flying around looking for the pollen needed to make honey. But when they need to be warriors, instinct takes over.

Without the honeybee, the earth around us would be desolate and bereft of fruit, vegetables, and flowers. It may be one of the smallest among God's creatures, but the function and purpose of the honeybee is vitally intertwined with the survival of mankind. Interestingly, as this book goes to press, there is a worldwide crisis concerning the honeybee, as whole swarms have been mysteriously dying off.

It was in 2005 that beekeepers in the United States started reporting a drastic reduction in their bee numbers, and in 2006, whole colonies started dying off, a phenomenon that became known as colony collapse disorder. There are numerous theories as to the causes of it, such as change in climate, disease, or the use of chemicals, but no one really knows for sure why it is happening. I believe this is a prophetic sign for us.

Never before has there been such a worldwide focus on and understanding of the importance of the honeybee. In this hour, the world is desperately crying out for the honeybee to arise as never before. Without the bee in its proper function, humans will grow weak, lacking the plants needed to nourish them, and the earth will be bereft of beauty and variety. The balance of earth's ecosystem is reliant upon this tiny creature thriving. Statistics from the US Department of Agriculture show that one third of the human diet comes both directly and indirectly from insect-pollinated plants, and honeybees account for eighty percent of this pollination.

I believe the very same thing is true in the church of God. At present, we are weakened and do not fully represent His power and glory as we were destined to do. The spirit of Deborah, the bee, must be released today to bring about pollination in the body of Christ and allow for the proper fruits, vegetables, and flowers to be grown for our nourishment and pleasure. I believe that Deborah lived in a prophetic anointing, the same prophetic anointing God wants to pour out over His girls in this hour.

There have been many thousands of women who have fought for the Lord throughout the years, and there is a baton ready to be passed on in this final part of the relay race of the ages. Are we willing to take up the torch and run with the anointing, in the fear of our God?

This is not about us and how strong and gifted we are; it is about God's timing, His desires, and His plans. Our part in this is to be willing to let Him transform and use us. It's not about personality or how brave or bold we may feel. If you were to meet me, you would probably be surprised. I'm not so scary, not so fierce, not really the warring type at all. I actually don't like conflict very much and prefer to do whatever is necessary to keep the peace.

In fact, I've always been pretty shy, and for a large part of my life, I was intensely bound up in fear. You name it and I've been afraid of it—especially people. Fear of man bound me so tightly that it has been a violent, bloody, and painful battle to get free from it. In some areas, I am still fighting. I have really felt like Gideon at times. I've asked the Lord, "How can You use *me*, so weak and afraid?" But God has been supernaturally moving in my life, transforming me and unveiling the hidden warrior within. Obedience is the key. If God says go, we go. I'm not much in myself, but in my God I am a powerful warrior, and when it comes to fighting in prayer, yes, I am fierce.

The warrior God wants to awaken within us is nothing less than the Spirit of God Himself. When we know the Father, we know the Warrior. The same power that raised Jesus from the dead lives inside of us. Our God is the Almighty, the Alpha and Omega. When He roars, His enemies scatter. We will not fight or overcome the enemy in our own authority but, rather, in the name of Jesus.

Women of God, it's time for us to stop looking at ourselves—our weaknesses and our strengths. Both are rooted in pride and self. Maybe you, like me, have struggled with believing that God could ever use you. You feel so wounded, weak, and afraid that just getting through the day is more than you can handle at times. Or maybe you've fallen into the other ditch, where you've hidden yourself behind your own cleverness and capabilities. You control your surroundings in order to protect yourself, so much so that God cannot break in. You have learned to fight and survive, but always in your own strength. Precious woman of God, let go and let God. It has never been about us, and it never will be.

None of us have what it takes to follow God by ourselves; it is all a gift of grace. Jesus is the Beginning and End of our qualifications and abilities. We were all unqualified and weak children, desperately in need of a Savior. When we understand this, we can then embrace our new identity, that of a true princess of royal blood and an heir to the kingdom of God. In Him, we are powerful, bound by love, and called to a life of destiny and meaning. If we are to rise up and fight in this hour, we must throw off our shackles of inferiority (and also of superiority) and arise in the spirit of true humility, fighting under the command and in the strength of the Lord Jesus Christ.

I believe that the times we are living in are sober and serious, yet they are full of suspense and glory. We do not know the day or the hour that Jesus will return, but the times tell us that His return is drawing ever closer. The church of God is living on the threshold of something so fantastic, so dramatic, that it is, as yet, hard for us to fathom.

Daniel, Joel, and John were among those who were given a glimpse into the future, and, as they all foresaw, the sons and daughters of God are about to be released as never before, to walk in the glory and light of the Lord. In these last days, there will be many great battles, because the enemy knows his time is running short, and his final fury is being unleashed against the bride of Christ.

In times of war and battle, it is an army, and not civilians, who are called upon to fight. Therefore, God must raise up His church to be an army made up of His sons and daughters. Joel was given a vision of this army, so awesome and so unrelenting:

Like dawn spreading across the mountains
   a large and mighty army comes,
such as never was of old
   nor ever will be in ages to come.
Before them fire devours,
   behind them a flame blazes.
Before them the land is like the garden of Eden,
   behind them, a desert waste —
nothing escapes them.
They have the appearance of horses;
   they gallop along like cavalry.
With a noise like that of chariots
   they leap over the mountaintops,
like a crackling fire consuming stubble,
   like a mighty army drawn up for battle.   Joel 2:2-5

Women of God, we have a place in this army. Are we willing to surrender and take our place?

Warrior Women, Arise!

Chapter 2

THE BELOVED WARRIOR

TO BECOME WARRIORS FOR JESUS, WE NEED TO know that we are the beloved daughters of God. We will fight for Him as a result of our love relationship, not because of force or fear. Even as the Father raises us up to be fierce warriors, He will hold us close to His heart, whispering words of love to us as we face every battle.

In order for an individual to develop properly, a foundation of love and security must be placed in the core of their being. A baby needs to be nourished and embraced with total love in order for this foundation to be laid. Any baby that does not experience this kind of love and nurturing will be affected for the rest of his or her life.

When we are born again and become babies in the kingdom, the same principle applies. Our Christian lives need to be founded on grace and a deep revelation of God's love for us. If we are to become warriors for Jesus, He wants to establish this truth in us: that we are His beloved.

The problem is that most of us didn't begin our natural or spiritual lives with a complete experience or understanding of the fact that we were unconditionally loved. Because of this, many of us have holes in our hearts that cause love to seep out, preventing it from ever really touching us. There is a love wound in the church today, as many of God's children struggle with believing that they are the beloved.

As women, a great number of us have a father wound, the result of our earthly fathers' failure to communicate to us that we were beloved daughters. They may have been absent, physically or emotionally. They may have been abusive, cold, angry, or passive. Or perhaps they simply did not have the ability or revelation to be able to communicate love to us in a way that we could receive. As a result, we daughters have grown up unsure of whether or not we were loved, and this wound often follows us into our relationship with our Father in heaven.

God wants to fill and heal us before we go out to war. He wants to give us a deeper revelation of His kind of love. It is an unconditional, eternal love, and it envelops and touches us to the very core of our spirits. Most important of all, God's love can never fail. Each one of us is radically loved by God, and He wants to enable us to receive this constant flow of love and then to let it pour out to others.

In order to do this, God needs to remove more and more sin, wounding, and fear from our lives. We love because He first loved us. We should never believe that we have to pump up this kind of love from within us; we must simply learn to receive love from the Father and allow His love to saturate and change us.

This whole concept of understanding God's love has always been a difficult one for me. When I first came to know Him, I struggled to believe that He could love me so unconditionally. I judged myself very harshly and expected Him to do likewise. Whenever I felt that I had failed in a certain area and was afraid that God was angry with me, I would withdraw from Him and hide (just as our mother Eve did in the garden so many years ago). In this way, I found myself cowering in a corner in my soul, like a hurt, trapped animal in a cage. I punished and rejected myself before God could do it, as I was certain this was how He would treat me.

Still, the farther I ran from my God, the deeper the longing grew in me to be found by Him. I began to discover that there was nowhere I could hide from His presence and love, and that He would always find and liberate me eventually. When I expected words of judgment and criticism, He would meet me with grace and kindness and an invitation to come into His presence. This would always lead me to run into His waiting arms and automatically repent of anything I needed to repent of. I have genuinely experienced the biblical truth that it is His *"kindness"* that *"leads* [us] *toward repentance"* (Romans 2:4).

We all have places inside our hearts that need to be healed and restored with the revelation of God's love. We may think that our healing is complete, but then He takes us even deeper into ourselves, and we recognize occasions in our lives when pain from the past resurfaced. It is at those times that we can allow ourselves to be placed on the operating table of the Holy Spirit. With the precision of a surgeon's knife, He can open up the wound, clean out all the infection, and then sew us up again. It is not fun, and it hurts, but is so necessary in order for us to be able to receive and walk in His love. If we do not allow the Father to heal us, the enemy keeps sticking his fingers into our wounds and causing us greater anguish.

Beelzebub is one of Satan's names, and it literally means "lord of the flies." Just as flies swarm to an open wound, so spiritual flies are attracted to the places of wounding in our lives. Let the Father heal you with His love.

All that Jesus did on behalf of the Father, when He walked on this earth, was motivated by love, and yet even He was given reassurance that He was the beloved. Just before He was sent into the desert to be tempted by Satan, God the Father spoke words of affirmation and love over His Son. As Jesus came up out of the water, after being baptized, He heard from heaven:

"This is my Son, whom I love; with him I am well pleased."   Matthew 3:17

Thus the Father affirmed His Son on earth and declared to all powers and principalities that Jesus was His beloved. Jesus could then enter into His time of temptation, emboldened by this knowledge.

Even Joan of Arc, who was one of the most fearless women warriors to ever walk the face of this earth, needed to hear words of comfort from her Father God before she could embrace the battle. When she cried out to Him in despair, during a time when her enemies were accusing her, He answered with the following words: "Child of God, go, go, go! I shall be with you to help you. Go!" [1]

This warrior needed to know that she was loved so that she could endure what lay ahead. And how much more do we also need that assurance? Allow the Father to touch you in the areas where you hide from Him or struggle to believe that He loves you. Even now He is hovering over you, longing to pour out His presence. Let the waves of His love crash over you and bring a fresh understanding of His heart for you. Then, as His beloved, you can become His warrior.

Warrior Women, Arise!

Chapter 3

OUR PLACE IN THE ARMY

God never planned for any woman to become a non-achiever or a failure in life. No woman was ever intended for prostitution or infidelity, for neglect or shame, for sickness or suffering, for destructiveness or non-productivity. No woman was ever destined by God to crawl in shame or to cower in a subservient role. Mary Magdalene was a vivid example. Jesus saw in her the strength of her resolve to believe in Him, even when the men retreated in seclusion after His crucifixion. They were afraid and were filled with unbelief. But Christ saw Mary's qualities. Others saw her past problems and her record as a demon-possessed woman. No wonder it amazed the disciples when Mary Magdalene was the one who brought them the news that Christ had risen and that she had seen the Lord. ... There are no limits for a woman who follows Christ.

— Daisy Washbourne Osborn [1]

GOD HAS DESIGNATED A SPECIAL TASK AND PLACE for each of us in His army. As warriors, it is time for us to find that place and then be trained for war. These terms may seem uncomfortable for many of us. We are used to thinking of war as something evil and destructive, and many times, in the flesh, it is. Instead, we want to be peacemakers, bringing God's love, kindness, and gentleness to this violent world. But the battle we are to fight is not of this world. Inside every one of us is a warrior, a fearless lioness, a fighter who shows her enemy no mercy and, instead, spreads terror in the camp of the enemy by her mere presence. Woman of God, this warrior is part of your identity, your inheritance, and your destiny.

In the film *Prince Caspian*, there is a scene in which Lucy meets Aslan. For those of you who don't know the story, Aslan is a talking lion who is also the true protector and ruler of the land of Narnia. Lucy is a young schoolgirl who, together with her older brothers and sister, has been transported through time into the land of Narnia, in order to save it from attack. She may be the youngest and, in many ways, the weakest of her family, but she has the ability to trust and to see Aslan, when others don't.

In this particular scene, Lucy has just ridden on horseback through dangerous enemy territory in order to seek Aslan's help. When she finally arrives, she and Aslan have the following conversation:

Lucy: I wish I could be braver.
Aslan: If you were any braver, you would be a lioness.

Lucy saw only her own weakness, but Aslan saw her through eyes of faith. He saw a young girl willing to fight, despite her fear, and this is the sign of true courage. Lucy was willing to ride alone through enemy territory in order to help her friends. Someone once said that true courage is not the absence of fear but the willingness to proceed in spite of it, and this is what Lucy did. Our Lord is not only a loving Savior, but He is also the Lord of Hosts. He is the Commander in Chief, a mighty warrior who has defeated all of His enemies. Jesus is the Lion of Judah, and as He roars, His enemies are scattered. And He has called us to stand at His side.

In a later scene in the same film, we see Lucy standing alone on a bridge, facing a massive enemy army. She stands there perfectly secure and at ease, but to the onlooker, the scene is absurd and terrifying. How can such a young girl stand a chance in the face of this merciless army? A few seconds later the scene changes, and we see Aslan, the lion, standing next to her. He then proceeds to roar, a roar that unleashes such power that it causes the waters to rise up, engulfing the enemy completely.

Lucy knew that Aslan was there with her all along, and that accounted for her total peace and confidence. The same is true for us in our lives. We have the Lion of Judah standing beside us, and when He roars, our enemies are defeated. To the world looking on, our simple faith may appear ridiculous and worthy of scorn. However, if Jesus leads us into battle, with and for Him, we can be utterly confident that He is standing beside us, ready to lead us to victory. Our role is simply to stand and trust:

"The Lord will fight for you; you need only to be still."

Exodus 14:14

We are made in the very image of God, and therefore we have the ability to fight and be victorious downloaded into our nature. Throw off all of your preconceived ideas about how you should behave as a woman of God, and let the lioness within you be released. It is time for us to let Jesus roar through us, time for us to shout. This is not about whether we are charismatic or not. It is not about personality; it is about us breaking through. We need to cry out for our own lives, for our families, for our cities, and for our nations.

The walls of Jericho came down with the shouts of the people of God. There are also some walls in your life and in the lives of people around you that will not come down unless you cry out to God. Shout to your Lord, cry out to Him, and watch the walls around you shatter:

Let the people of Sela sing for joy;
let them shout from the mountaintops.
Let them give glory to the Lord
and proclaim his praise in the islands.
The Lord will march out like a mighty man,
like a warrior he will stir up his zeal;
with a shout he will raise the battle cry
and will triumph over his enemies.
"For a long time I have kept silent,
I have been quiet and held myself back.

OUR PLACE IN THE ARMY

But now, like a woman in childbirth,
  I cry out, I gasp and pant."   Isaiah 42:11-14

I believe that God is sending forth a battle cry across the earth today, for it is time for the sons and daughters of glory to be revealed.

Many of us have been quiet for a long time, and in some cases, God Himself has kept us back, while He was doing a work of refining and reshaping in us. But now is the time for release, the time for us to cry out like a woman in childbirth. I believe that God wants to birth something new on this earth, and we can be part of what He is doing.

As any of us who have given birth know, it is a painful, exhausting, and messy process. At the same time, there is nothing so exhilarating and honoring as to be chosen to deliver a new life into the world. As women, we are designed to call forth things in the natural and in the spiritual. We can pray forth the will of God and see His plans be formed, grow, and even come to fruition.

The Lord is raising the battle cry. Are you willing to sign up for His army? Are you willing to let Him teach you to fight, to let Him train you for war?

A revolution is coming in which good will prevail and overcome evil. The people of God will be seen for who they truly are, and the words of Isaiah will echo among us:

"Arise, shine, for your light has come,
  and the glory of the Lord rises upon you.

39

See, darkness covers the earth
  and thick darkness is over the peoples,
but the LORD rises upon you
  and his glory appears over you."   Isaiah 60:1-2

We all have heavenly assignments, designed especially for us, to accomplish. The battles that the Lord will lead us into will be both individual and corporate. Perhaps He is calling you into politics, the media, the arts, education, the business world, motherhood, missionary work, or church ministry. It could be that He is asking you to be faithful in the area of responsibility He has already given you. Possibly He is calling you to a secret life of prayer, in which He alone is your reward. Whatever area of society and responsibility God has called you to, be faithful in the small things, seek Him for your destiny, and dare to call forth your hidden desires, dreams, or prophecies.

Some of you may have allowed dust and cobwebs to cover the promises of God for your life. You have allowed the enemy and the cares of this world to bury the treasure of God within you. Have you permitted unbelief and disillusionment to quench the words God spoke to you in your youth because of the delay you have suffered in seeing the fulfillment of those promises? Perhaps those around you have so scorned your dreams and faith that you have even lost hope yourself, overcome with cynicism and self-doubt. You may be one who knows and believes the plans of God for you, but you are unsure as to how to pursue or fulfill them. Precious women of God, "[He] *is not a man, that he should lie*" (Numbers 23:19). If God has spoken about your life, then His word stands strong. He is *"the same yesterday and today and forever"* (Hebrews 13:8).

This is the hour of the fulfillment of God's promises. We need to rise up and take hold of that which He has promised us before the beginning of time. The only person who can hold you back from fulfilling your destiny is you yourself. The hordes of hell may be sent against you, and men may revile, abuse, and mock, but the purpose of God for you stands strong. Nothing can separate you from God's love (see Romans 8:38-39). You are more than a conqueror through Christ Jesus (see Romans 8:37), and *"no weapon that is formed against you will prosper"* (Isaiah 54:17, NASB). All you have to do is simply agree with God's truth about you. Surrender all your unbelief, fear, and lack of trust. Give Him your disappointments, bitterness, anger, pride, and failures. Get honest with God. Draw near to Him, and He will draw near to you.

We are all called to fight, but we cannot all fight the same battles. It is time for us to find our place in the army of God, humbly accepting the position our Great Commander gives us. Our reward will not be based on the apparent greatness or influence of our position, but, rather, on our obedience and trust. We will all receive the same reward—if we are faithful—no matter what position we are to hold here upon earth:

"The share of the man who stayed with the supplies is to be the same as that of him who went down to battle. All will share alike." 1 Samuel 30:24

The story of Deborah and Jael is an encouraging example of this. Judges 4 describes how Deborah, the leader, judge, and mother over Israel, went out to battle against the enemies of the nation. She helped to lead the armies into war, along with Barak, both physically and through the prophetic words of guidance she received from the Lord. The result was that all of the enemy troops were killed. Still, their commanding officer, a man named Sisera, managed to escape. It was not Deborah, Barak, or any other member of the armies of Israel who ultimately killed Sisera, but a simple tent-dwelling woman (a housewife, in modern terms) named Jael.

This woman skillfully and courageously lured Sisera into her tent and gave him some milk to drink. Then, as he lay sleeping, she drove a tent peg into his temple, killing him (see Judges 4:18-21). Thus, the honor for victory in that battle went, ultimately, to a relatively unknown woman.

You may not be called to be one who leads and judges. You may not be a prophetess who finds it easy to hear the voice of the Lord. You may not have influence and power in society to affect thousands of people. You may not be known at all. You could be a faithful housewife, tending to your children and your family, a school teacher, cleaner, businesswoman, waitress, or grandmother, fulfilling everyday tasks with faithful diligence. Yet your hour of glory is waiting around the next corner, where God may allow you to be used to conquer His enemies with a simple act of bravery. Perhaps you will one day be known as Jael was:

"Most blessed of women be Jael,
the wife of Heber the Kenite,
most blessed of tent-dwelling women."   Judges 5:24

Your act of kindness, boldness, witness, or love may change lives around you today, and may even affect the destiny of your people and nation.

During World War II, a woman named Miep Gies hid Anne Frank and her family in a secret attic annex in Amsterdam, Holland, for more than two years before the Nazis eventually discovered them. This woman put her life at risk daily in order to feed and protect the Frank family. She was an ordinary member of society who made a righteous choice to defy the evil system at work at the time. She is quoted as saying, "Imagine young people would grow up with the feeling that you have to be a hero to do your human duty. I am afraid nobody would ever help other people, because who is a hero? I was not. I was just an ordinary housewife and secretary." [2]

But that seemingly small and insignificant choice has influenced the course of history. Miep kept the writings of Anne Frank, which later became published in book form as *The Diaries of Anne Frank,* and this book has been circulated throughout the world and been read by millions of people. It gives insight into the terror of those times and stands as a constant reminder of what was done to the Jewish people, and it continues to inspire us to fight for justice and peace in our world.

Anne Frank was only a young girl when she wrote her dairy, yet she had a longing to impact the world through her writings. In her dairy entry for Wednesday, April 5, 1944, she wrote, "I finally realized that I must do my schoolwork to keep from being ignorant, to get on in life, to become a journalist, because that's what I want! I know I can write ... , but it remains to be seen whether I really have talent.

"And if I don't have the talent to write books or newspaper articles, I can always write for myself. But I want to achieve more than that. I can't imagine living like Mother, Mrs. van Daan, and all the women who go about their work and are then forgotten. I need to have something besides a husband and children to devote myself to! ...

"I want to be useful or bring enjoyment to all people, even those I've never met. I want to go on living even after my death! And that's why I'm so grateful to God for having given me this gift, which I can use to develop myself and to express all that's inside me! When I write, I can shake off all my cares. My sorrow disappears, my spirits are revived. But, and that's a big question, will I ever be able to write something great, will I ever become a journalist or a writer?" [3]

Anne Frank asked herself this question, and then she died in a concentration camp, never having learned the answer. Still, her words became a self-fulfilling prophecy, and she goes on living even after her death. Miep Gies and Anne Frank were both Jaels, women who courageously embraced their opportunity to drive a tent peg into the temple of their enemy.

The name *Jael* actually stems from the Hebrew word which means "to ascend, to be valuable, useful." It may be your time to ascend to the heights of your destiny and there to receive revelation that you are valuable and useful to God and His kingdom. In fact, you have been all along.

Jael's name belonged to her even before she acted upon it. Rise up to the circumstances God places you in, and let that which already exists within you be released. Thank God that He does not look at the outward appearance but, rather, *"looks at the heart"* (1 Samuel 16:7). Thank God that He chooses to use *"the foolish things of the world to shame the wise"* and *"the weak things of the world to shame the strong"* (1 Corinthians 1:27-29).

If you are not called to be one who stands before other people, don't be jealous or idolize the position of one who does. If you do so, you may miss God's opportunity and destiny for yourself. Rather, we must work together as a team, each of us running the particular race God has given us. If we each stay in our own lane, without trying to push and shove, then we can all complete the race set before us. Then Jesus will be glorified, and victory will result.

45

Again the prophet Joel foresaw an army that looked like this, and he said of that army:

> *At the sight of them, nations are in anguish;*
>   *every face turns pale.*
> *They charge like warriors;*
>   *they scale walls like soldiers.*
> *They all march in line,*
>   *not swerving from their course.*
> *They do not jostle each other;*
>   *each marches straight ahead.*
> *They plunge through defenses*
>   *without breaking ranks.*   Joel 2:6-8

This is what God's warrior bride will look like, each in position, focused on the ultimate goal—to glorify Jesus.

This army will be made up of both men and women and both young and old, but we will all be fighting as one unified force. In this hour, I believe that the Spirit of God is calling His girls to take their place in this mighty army.

If you know that God is calling you to be a leader, then embrace that calling fully. Don't let false humility hold you back. Don't say, "Surely not me, Lord! I could never lead, never be used to boldly speak Your Word!" If He has called you, it is for His name's sake.

The church, the armies of God, and the Baraks of this present world need you. In fact, I believe the words from Deborah's song echo prophetically today:

"Then the people of the LORD
went down to the city gates.
'Wake up, wake up, Deborah!
Wake up, wake up, break out in song!' "

Judges 5:11-12

There is a battle to be fought, and I believe that the anointing of Deborah prepares the way for other women to dare to step into their destiny and act, just as Jael did. Neither Deborah nor Jael was any better than the other. They had different purposes, yet both were faithful to their calling. This is the desire of our Father for each one of us. The enemy and our own insecurities and pride deceive and hold us back, tempting us to compare, envy, and judge. But who are we to judge the Lord's anointed? If He has called you, submit. If He has called your sister, release and bless her. Let the spirit of competition and envy die in the fire of God. Each one of us is necessary. In fact, we must rely on one another if victory is to be won.

Warrior Women, Arise!

Chapter 4

THE NATURE OF THE BATTLE

If you know the enemy and know yourself, you need not fear the result of a hundred battles. If you know yourself but not the enemy, for every victory gained you will also suffer a defeat. If you know neither the enemy nor yourself, you will succumb in every battle.

— Sun Tzu, *The Art of War* [1]

ONE DAY I WENT TO PICK UP MY YOUNGEST SON, Daniel, from school. As I walked into the classroom, he caught sight of me and came running toward me. He was about halfway to me when another boy in the class stuck out his foot and tripped him. Daniel fell to the floor, hurt his face, and burst into tears. Almost immediately, however, he picked himself up and ran into my arms, and I was able to comfort him.

At the time, I didn't give this much thought, although I was, of course, saddened that it had happened. Later in the week, however, when I was brushing my teeth and thinking about the battle we find ourselves in, I was reminded of that event and how it had unfolded. I sensed that, as God's children, life for us is often as it was for Daniel that day. We are running toward God, seeking His presence and security, but on our way there the enemy sticks out his foot and tries to trip us. He does everything in his power to keep us from getting to the Father.

When the enemy succeeds in tripping us, we lie there on the floor, away from God and hurting, and it is our attitude and decision at that moment that determines whether the enemy will have the victory or not. If we continue to lie there feeling sorry for ourselves and allowing bitterness and hopelessness to fill us, we will be defeated. We may even allow thoughts like these to consume us:

"What's the point of trying to get to know God?
You just get hurt in the process."
"Seeking God only leads to more and more pain."

We may even blame God, at times, for tripping us.

It is in this place of self-pity and doubt that the enemy wants to keep us. However, if we quickly get up off the floor, as Daniel did, and run into the Father's embrace, we will be safe. He can then comfort us, speaking tender words of love to us. In His arms, the fall will be forgotten, and we will attain our original goal, namely, to get closer to our God.

There are many ways in which the enemy tries to trip us up, through broken relationships, sickness, rejection, fear, temptation, and deception. The list is endless. We cannot always control whether or not the enemy will try to trip us, but we can control our reaction to his treachery. If we will get up and run into the arms of God, we will know His love, healing, comfort, and heart for us in a deeper way than if we had never been tripped in the first place. In this way, we can turn the attacks of the enemy into victories for our lives and use them to deepen and strengthen our relationship with our Creator. God hates to see us get tripped, just as I hated seeing my son fall and get hurt, yet He loves to hold and comfort us when we run to Him in our time of need.

This illustration helps to define the nature of the battle that we, as believers, find ourselves in. The battle we are to fight *"is not against flesh and blood"*:

> *For our struggle is not against flesh and blood, but against the rulers, against the authorities, against the powers of this dark world and against the spiritual forces of evil in the heavenly realms.*   Ephesians 6:12

Satan is our enemy. He hates us with a vengeance, and his aim is *"to steal and kill and destroy"* (John 10:10). He is the father of lies, deceit, and disunity. He *"prowls around like a roaring lion looking for someone to devour"* (1 Peter 5:8). He comes *"as an angel of light,"* deceiving with apparent delight (2 Corinthians 11:14). In all of this, his goal is to steal mankind's worship of and relationship with God.

Satan is our enemy through and through, and in him there is no mercy, grace, or love. It is against him and his hordes of hell that our battle lies. Too often we have been tricked into seeing our fellow human beings as the ultimate enemy. Although it is true that many times Satan works through other people in order to wound and destroy us, ultimately the battle lies on a deeper plane.

It may be natural to want to lash out at those who have hurt us and to see them as our enemies, but when we do so, the battle is lost. When we fight in the natural, victory can never fully be achieved. It is only through prayer and battling in the heavenlies that true spiritual victory can be released. We must fight, not as the world fights, with guns and power, but with the weapons God has given us. We must fight through establishing God's truth in our minds and proclaiming it:

> *For though we live in the world, we do not wage war as the world does. The weapons we fight with are not the weapons of the world. On the contrary, they have divine power to demolish strongholds.* 2 Corinthians 10:3-4

From the moment of conception, every human being is thrown into a war zone, whether they are aware of it or not. The battle has begun, the battle for our lives, our souls, our destinies. For each new life being formed in the womb, there is a battle for fatherhood. The heavenly Father knows us in the womb, and He creates us according to His image. There he downloads into us gifts, talents, and anointings. He places destinies in our hearts, a deposit of Himself, which we can chose to seek after and find as we grow:

> *For you created my inmost being;*
> *you knit me together in my mother's womb.*

My frame was not hidden from you
  when I was made in the secret place.
When I was woven together in the depths of the earth,
  your eyes saw my unformed body.
All the days ordained for me
  were written in your book
  before one of them came to be.

Psalm 139:13 and 15-16

At the same time, Satan, the father of lies, unleashes his plan, attempting to quench our life, even in the womb, a strategy he has been horrendously successful with. (It is estimated that forty-six million babies are aborted annually worldwide). If Satan can't kill us, he attempts to implant into us lies and wounding through our mother's emotions or circumstances surrounding her pregnancy. He wants us to believe that we are not wanted, loved, or accepted, even before we enter this world physically.

Satan wants to father us with control, lies, and deception, not because he cares for us, but because he wants to hurt God, our Creator. Satan can wound the heart of the only true Father by destroying His children or even turning them against Him. Satan knows the Father, for he has stood in His presence and worshiped Him and has seen His glory and His power. He knows the intensity of the love of God and also understands that he has no power to face off with God. He and his hordes were violently cast out of heaven and will never enter it again:

And there was war in heaven. Michael and his angels fought against the dragon, and the dragon and his angels fought back. But he was not strong enough, and they lost their place in heaven. The great dragon was hurled down—that ancient serpent called the devil, or Satan, who leads the whole world astray. He was hurled to the earth, and his angels with him. Revelation 12:7-9

This passage goes on to explain that Satan is enraged at being hurled down. He also knows that his time is short, and so he roams about like a trapped wild beast, determined to make war against the church:

Then the dragon was enraged at the woman and went off to make war against the rest of her offspring—those who obey God's commandments and hold to the testimony of Jesus. Revelation 12:17

In the face of God, the enemy is powerless, defenseless. However, he can exert influence over the hearts and minds of God's creation and, thereby, gain authority on the earth. He saw his chance when Adam and Eve were created. Through them, he could enter into God's world and seek to destroy it.

Satan knows that God would never control or demand love, so when he came to Eve and tried to deceive her, his tactic was to lure her into doubting her Creator's words and commands. Satan won that battle and gained access to this world, managing to cause a rift between God and His creation.

But God can never be outsmarted, and He had already made provision for a solution to the Fall. When God sent Jesus, the consequences of that fateful day in Eden were reversed, and Jesus now makes a way for mankind to once again stand boldly in God's presence, in spite of his sinful nature and his weaknesses:

God made you alive with Christ. He forgave us all our sins, having canceled the written code, with its regulations, that was against us and that stood opposed to us; he took it away, nailing it to the cross. And having disarmed the powers and authorities, he made a public spectacle of them, triumphing over them by the cross.

Colossians 2:13-15

Satan's power is destroyed, and he is a defeated foe. However, he continues to use his oldest tactic against us—deception. He seeks to deceive God's crowning creation, man, so that he will not understand what Jesus has done for him. Satan wants to keep the revelation of what Jesus did for us veiled, so that even those who believe in Him will never truly enter into their destiny or see their place of authority over the enemy. He tries to keep us from entering into our full inheritance, where we are promised total freedom and intimacy with our Creator. Satan continues to lie to us day and night, seeking to wear down the saints and hold us in bondage.

The first level of our battle, as warriors, therefore, is to allow the Holy Spirit to restore truth to our minds and, using it, to shake off the deception and bondage the enemy has attempted to implant in us and place upon us:

We demolish arguments and every pretension that sets itself up against the knowledge of God, and we take captive every thought to make it obedient to Christ.

2 Corinthians 10:5

How many of us can truly say that we are walking in the full revelation and glory of our heavenly Father? How many of us are convinced that the same power that raised Jesus from the dead dwells in us (see Ephesians 1:18-20)? How many of us are one hundred percent convinced that the Lord is totally for us, and not against us (see Romans 8:31), and that nothing we do or do not do can affect His love and commitment to us? How many of us, if we were to stand face to face with Satan, would be secure that *"greater is he that is in* [us], *than he that is in the world"* (1 John 4:4, KJV)? I would dare to venture that across the world there are few who could answer with a bold yes to all these questions. Whether we want to face it or not, we have all been deceived, bound up, and held back, some to a greater degree than others, but no one has been totally untouched by the enemy's deceit. We have found ourselves in a bloody battle, the battle for our minds.

Jesus has said that He will return for a pure and spotless bride, which means there is much work to be done.

I believe that the hour has come when God will begin to remove all deception, lies, and unbelief from His church. The veil over our minds and hearts will be pulled back, and we will begin to see and understand the things of God as never before. The Spirit of understanding, revelation, and wisdom will be released throughout God's church, and His children will begin to behold their Father in heaven as He truly is.

We cannot enter into battle against Satan when we do not truly believe we can defeat him, and we cannot defeat him if we don't believe the Lord of Hosts is for us. It is vital for us to understand the power of the cross, that on it Jesus crucified all sin, sickness, powers, and principalities (and even death itself), and that He now is a resurrected Conqueror who offers us new life.

At the cross, Jesus replaced our sickness with His healing, our sin with His forgiveness and cleansing, death with eternal life, a life of defeat with victory, and estrangement from God with unhindered intimacy. Most of us have understood this with our intellect but still live our daily lives distanced from the reality of what Jesus has won for us. Only the Holy Spirit can reveal these truths to us and imprint them upon our hearts.

Women of God, isn't it time for us to throw off all unbelief and *"the sin that so easily entangles"* (Hebrews 12:1) and to cry out for this revelation? Cry out to God for fire, His all-consuming fire that will burn away all doubts, fears, unbelief, lukewarmness, and compromise. He is ready and waiting to help us, so run boldly into His arms and ask Him for help today.

For too long we have been enslaved by fear, intimidation, and weakness. The enemy has held the women of God in chains of iron. It is time for us to break out and cry out for freedom—freedom for our souls, freedom for our minds, freedom for our families, and freedom for our nations. Satan has bitten our heel, but we are called to crush his head, as we boldly walk into battle, with the Lion of Judah leading the way. We are invincible in the power of our Lord, *"not by might, nor by power, but by* [His] *Spirit"* (Zechariah 4:6).

Women of God, rise up and see your enemy for who he really is. He will not leave you alone just because you are weak or hurting, for he has no mercy. Ed Silvoso writes in his book *Women, God's Secret Weapon*, "It is the devil who has to watch out, since he is the one described with a bruised head. While women walk upright, Satan must always crawl, making his head vulnerable every time they set their feet down. He is the one who should be afraid, not the other way around." [2]

He continues, "Women need to discover this truth. The devil knows that God does not lie. What God promises always comes to pass. This is why Satan has spent centuries belittling women and weaving a web of lies into a formidable worldwide network of oppression to hold them down. He knows that when women find out who they really are, his evil kingdom will come to an abrupt end. He cannot afford to have women walking upright. He desperately needs to keep them down." [3]

Therefore, let us rise up and walk, with our heads held high, knowing who we are in God. Our Father wants to take back what has been stolen from us and restore the years the enemy has ravaged from us.

The cry for freedom is resounding in the air. The prison many of us are sitting in is not even real. It is built of deception and unbelief. The Father sent Jesus to set the captives free nearly two thousand years ago, so you don't belong in a prison. Princess of God, your Knight in shining armor has already been sent to free you:

For he has rescued us from the dominion of darkness and brought us into the kingdom of the Son he loves, in whom we have redemption, the forgiveness of sins.

Colossians 1:13-14

The dragon is slain, and you are free to go. Walk out of the tower today. Your Prince has been waiting for you all these years, waiting for you to realize what He has done for you. Shake off the dust that has attached itself to you, and break out of your shackles, for you are free:

Awake, awake, O Zion,
  clothe yourself with strength.
Put on your garments of splendor,
  O Jerusalem, the holy city.
The uncircumcised and defiled
  will not enter you again.
Shake off your dust;

rise up, sit enthroned, O Jerusalem.
Free yourself from the chains on your neck,
   O captive Daughter of Zion.   Isaiah 52:1-2

Woman of God, you are God's princess. Your royal robe is one of righteousness, your crown is the mind of Christ, and your scepter of authority is His blood. He has placed a seal over your heart. You are royalty, fully and legally adopted into His kingdom. Therefore, this is your hour to shine, to accomplish the tasks He decided for you before the beginning of time. Your destiny is calling.

Warrior Women, Arise!

Chapter 5

THE BATTLE WITHIN

THE BATTLE IN WHICH WE FIND OURSELVES TAKES place on two fronts: There is the evil around us, as well as the sin nature within us. We know that we have the Spirit and the flesh battling within us and that Jesus wants us to live our lives led by the Spirit. Paul describes this battle and even gives advice as to how to fight it successfully:

So I say, live by the Spirit, and you will not gratify the desires of the sinful nature. For the sinful nature desires what is contrary to the Spirit, and the Spirit what is contrary to the sinful nature. They are in conflict with each other, so that you do not do what you want. But if you are led by the Spirit, you are not under law.

Galatians 5:16-18

We know that we have two seeds warring within us — the seed of Adam and the seed of Christ. It is through being constantly filled with God's Spirit that we overcome, not by focusing on changing our own behavior or following a set of rules and regulations which the Bible calls *"the law."* Jesus has now written His law upon our hearts, and as we come closer to Him and surrender our wills, we will find ourselves wanting to follow Him and His ways. We live in a fallen world and will continue to do so until our Lord makes all things new, but Jesus commands us to pray that "[His] *Kingdom come*" and "[His] *will be done on earth as it is in heaven*" (Matthew 6:10). He wants to reveal His kingdom here on this earth, and He has chosen to use His followers to do this.

We can reflect the glory of God here on earth, even in our broken, fallen state. How? The darkness is all around us, but we are called to shine as lights in the midst of that darkness. In these times of battle, our greatest weapon and defense is to allow God's Spirit to truly rule in our lives. The Lord is looking for true disciples who will freely give themselves to Him, living sacrifices who will offer their own desires, will, and plans and surrender to the all-consuming fire of God. He is looking for people who will allow Him to purge away the dross until all that remains in them is pure gold.

Kathryn Kuhlman was a powerful evangelist, a woman used mightily by God in healing and miracles during the 1950s and 1960s. The message that permeated and dominated her ministry was one of surrender. She understood that in order for God to work His miraculous power through us, there is a need for the total submission of our wills, our desires—our everything. She once described how she was forced to make a heart-wrenching decision of whether or not to surrender the man she loved (who, she knew, she was not supposed to be with) and to follow her heavenly Love. She walked along a dark alley one night, wrestling with God, and came to a sign in the road which read "Dead End." She described her response to seeing this sign: "There was heartache, heartache so great it cannot be put into words. If you think it is easy to go to the cross, it's simply because you've never been there. I've been there. I know. And I had to go alone. I knew nothing about the wonderful filling of the Holy Spirit. I knew nothing about the power of the mighty third person of the Trinity which was available to all. I just knew it was four o'clock on Saturday afternoon and I had come to a place in my life where I was ready to give up everything—even Mister—and die. I said it out loud: "Dear Jesus, I surrender all. I give it all to you. Take my body. Take my heart. All I am is yours. I place it in your wonderful hands." [1] The anointing and power she walked in during the latter years of her life was a direct result of her decision to surrender her will totally to the Father. She was just one woman who made this choice, but her life impacted thousands, if not millions, of lives, and her legacy remains to this day.

Are any of us willing to pick up the baton she left behind and run with it? Who among us is willing to live as a bond servant of the Lord, fully submitted to His will? The process may be painful at times, but the end result will far outweigh any suffering we might experience. The battle against our flesh is won as we submit, for there is no longer any need to fight once your enemy is dead and buried.

Woman of God, hear the heart of your Father and Lord in this. He is not out to control or destroy you in His wrath; He is offering you a life of glory and power in His love. He is wooing His girls, calling them to come closer. Your destiny is to be transformed into the likeness of His presence, to be like Jesus—to talk like Him, walk like Him, act like Him.

He can be likened to a father who wishes to give his newly adopted daughter a gift of ice cream, but all she knows from the orphanage is the filthy piece of bread in her hand. She cannot receive the ice cream unless she lets go of the bread. There is no room in her hands for both. She is afraid to lose the bread, which has been all she has known and depended on for survival, but unless she lets go of that which she knows, she cannot receive the gift of the father.

This describes our situation. Many times we are afraid to let go of the things in our lives that actually harm us or that bring us no joy. They are all we know, and they give us a false sense of security. We have dug our own wells, looking to false gods to meet our needs, but these leave us even more empty and thirsty:

> *"My people have committed two sins:*
> *They have forsaken me,*
> *the spring of living water,*
> *and have dug their own cisterns,*
> *broken cisterns that cannot hold water."*
>
> Jeremiah 2:13

Faith requires us to leave our broken cisterns and embrace the gift of the Father, but we cannot receive the Father's gifts without emptying our hands.

Precious daughter of God, the Father wants to pour out His blessings and gifts upon you. Are you willing to let go of the things you are holding onto—your fear, your insecurity, your areas of weakness, whatever the Holy Spirit is shining His light upon? He will not and cannot share you with another, and the fullness of His light and glory can only shine through a surrendered vessel. We can overcome the sin nature, as we drink from the well of God on a consistent basis and allow His Spirit to saturate and transform us.

We each have our own battles to fight, in various areas of our lives, but the battle is not just about us; the battle is also about those millions of men, women, and children, both within and outside the church, who are in bondage. It is for the peoples of the earth, whom the Father has given to Jesus as His inheritance. Who will cry out for them? Who will set them free from slavery? Who will fight for them?

The Spirit of the Lord searches throughout the earth day and night, and He sees everything. God sees the pain in the hearts of men. He sees all sickness, death, injustice, desperation, loneliness, hopelessness, anger, abuse, fear, doubt, debt, greed, hatred, strife, sexual immorality, and violence. He weeps, He grieves, and His holy anger erupts against the sins of man.

The most tragic thing of all is that God has already provided an answer for these things in Jesus. He has given of Himself, given that which was most precious to Him, and still the world rejects Him. Not only that, but those who claim to believe in Him walk mostly in spiritual poverty and unbelief. They have *"a form of godliness,"* but, at the same time, they are *"denying its power"* (2 Timothy 3:5).

God is looking for those who are willing to humble themselves, stand up, get into position, and cry out for those in need (see Ezekiel 22:30 and 2 Chronicles 7:14). Woman of God, are you willing to have the heart of Esther, who had the boldness and courage to stand before her king, even if it cost her life, and plead for the lives of a people about to be extinguished? Millions of people lie before us right now, whom the enemy has planned to annihilate from the face of this earth and to take with him into an eternity of hell. What will be our response?

Esther was one woman, an orphan whom God raised up and made queen. She was one woman who had no power or influence herself, but whom the Lord exalted and crowned with glory and power, and whose actions changed the destiny of a nation, Israel.

I am sure that Esther struggled with thoughts of fear, doubt, and inferiority. She may have wondered who she was to go before the king, just as you may struggle with your assignment today. But Esther saw beyond herself and her fears, even beyond her blessings and position. She saw destiny. She saw that perhaps she was there *"for such a time as this"* (Esther 4:14). God gave her the eyes of faith and the ability to trust. She went boldly before the throne, and the king extended to her the scepter, just as our King in heaven extends the heavenly scepter to us today.

In those days, it was illegal for anyone to enter the king's presence without him first calling for them, and the sentence for breaking this law was death. If, however, the king extended his scepter, it represented his grace, and the life of that person was spared, and he or she was permitted to speak.

The same applies to us today. Because of sin, we could not enter the Lord's presence without incurring the penalty of death, but He has extended His holy scepter to us through Jesus. Now we are free to enter into His throne room whenever we choose and plead for His mercy for our own lives and the lives of others.

Esther was a warrior, and her weapon was intercession. She dared to stand in the gap for thousands of others and plead their cause. Daughter of God, you are not an orphan. You are not alone, weak, and without hope:

"For I know the plans I have for you," declares the LORD, "plans to prosper you and not to harm you, plans to give you hope and a future." Jeremiah 29:11

Submit to His treatment, relinquish your sin nature, and allow Him to anoint you. Seek His plan for your life. Cry out to Him for the lost around you. Your willingness to trust, to speak, and to pray can change lives. You are called to be a warrior, a history-maker. Enter into the battle for freedom, yours and others', and see the victory the Lord will give you.

Warrior Women, Arise!

Chapter 6

THE BATTLE IS NOT AGAINST MEN

The first sin created a gap between man and woman, the gender gap which is the oldest horizontal gap. Since that sad day in the Garden, men and women have suffered its consequences, the most devastating of which is the utter state of incompleteness for both of them when they do not walk in harmony. This in turn has handed the devil a tremendous advantage. Never has the axiom "divide and conquer" rendered higher dividends than when Satan applied it to the gender gap.

— Ed Silvoso [1]

IN ALL THIS DISCUSSION ABOUT WOMEN BEING raised up, I want to clarify and proclaim that this rising up is not to be in a spirit of feminism, anger, and revolt against men. Men are not our enemies, and the battle is not against them. However, there is a wound between us, one that was first felt some six thousand years ago with Adam and Eve.

God created us in His image, man and woman, each of us reflecting an important side of His character. We were created to work together as a team, our lives beautifully intertwined in openness, passion, and task. Adam and Eve were commissioned to be fruitful and increase in number, fill the earth and subdue it. Their lives, their destinies, even their bodies were intertwined with each other in total openness and trust. They knew that they needed each other. Here the enemy saw his chance to destroy and tried to drive a wedge between them.

Eve succumbed to this temptation, taking control in the relationship, and Adam gave way to passivity and did not stand up to protect them both. He allowed himself to be controlled and manipulated by his woman. The result ... well, any of us who are married or have ever had any contact with men know the result. We are like two separate entities. We can misunderstand, disappoint, frustrate, and, at our worst, abuse one another.

Satan has twisted God's perfect plan for men and women. He hates the unity and image of God they represent. He saw Adam and Eve in their undefiled state, and he knows the unbeatable foe they represent together. Therefore, he has pitted them against each other.

The battle between men and women is real, and it is bloody, but it is not against flesh and blood. We are both caught in the crossfire in this war. Satan has used men and their systems of politics, power, and corruption to suppress and subdue women. Men, in their fallen state, have allowed themselves to be used to commit unthinkable crimes against the bodies, souls, and hearts of women.

We women, however, are not without blame. We, too, have used the weapons of control, manipulation, sexual power, and cunning to disarm and emasculate the hearts of men. Thus, men and women alike have freely allowed themselves to be used as pawns in the chess match of the ages.

God created marriage as a gift and picture of the intimacy and respect between Jesus and His church. No wonder the enemy has sought to defile and degrade it so! In fact, Satan is the only one (besides God) who has seen men, women, and the Father existing together in complete transparency, wholeness, and purity. He saw the image of God reflected magnificently in Adam and Eve, as they existed in the state in which they were intended to live, without sickness, fear, suffering, or any other consequence of sin. He saw man and woman living out their inheritance together, walking with and talking to their Creator face to face. He saw it all, and I'm sure the memories of that perfection and true harmony plague him even to this day, inciting him to continue to sow seeds of enmity and strife between men and women and their God.

I feel confident that all of you women reading this book have been wounded by men at some time and in some way or form. The wound is there, and for many of us it has penetrated deeply. You may have been sexually, physically, verbally, or spiritually abused by a man, and the effect of the abuse remains to haunt and deter you in your walk with the Lord.

Your wounds may have come in your everyday interactions with men, through their degrading comments, lustful looks, or discriminatory actions in the workplace or even in the church. Perhaps that wound has even caused you to stop trusting your heavenly Father. You may have found yourself reasoning:

"Jesus is, after all, a man. Won't He be like all the others?"

The enemy has cleverly used men to inflict the damage he wants to bring about, a wound to our sexuality, beauty, calling, and identity. But our battle is not against men; it is against the forces of hell that have been sent against mankind (men and women alike) to keep us from entering into the freedom and life Christ won for us.

Still, what do we do with the men in our lives who have been used to inflict these wounds? Such a wound may have developed into bitterness and hate, which, like an unwelcome infection, seep their way into our bloodstream, slowly poisoning our whole being with their filth. Forgiveness is the weapon Jesus offers us, as warrior women. This is the key to opening the door to our healing and reconciliation with men, as well as the key to setting others free.

Jesus was very clear on this issue. In no uncertain terms, He commanded us to forgive:

"For if you forgive men when they sin against you, your heavenly Father will also forgive you. But if you do not forgive men their sins, your Father will not forgive your sins." Matthew 6:14-15

To the wounded, this command can appear to add even more pain to an already painful situation. Some may even ask questions such as:

"Doesn't God understand how much it hurts?"
"Does He not see what was done to me?"

How do you tell a woman in Uganda who watched her husband being brutally murdered and then was subjected to rape and other physical abuse, to forgive the men who committed these horrendous acts? Where is the compassion and empathy of God? This is how the human mind reasons, but forgiveness is foundational to the redemption and reconciliation of mankind—with God and each other. It is a bridge over which the grace and healing of God can reach us.

Corrie ten Boom was a woman who used this weapon of forgiveness most courageously. During World War II she and her family chose to help, even hide, numerous Jews in Holland who were being persecuted. She was eventually imprisoned for this, along with her sister, Betsie. Enduring much hardship and suffering in concentration camps, she and her sister consistently chose to trust God in the midst of their trials and spread the love of God to those around them.

Betsie died in prison, while Corrie survived, and after the war she would often speak at various Christian gatherings. Her message was saturated with forgiveness and hope, and she was a much-needed voice speaking to a post-war generation.

Corrie was herself tested in this area of forgiveness when, while speaking in Germany, she was approached by a former SS officer who had been a guard at Ravensbruck, where she had been imprisoned. She describes this meeting in her book *The Hiding Place*: "His hand was thrust out to shake mine. And I, who had preached so often to the people of Bloemendaal the need to forgive, kept my hand at my side.

"Even as the angry, vengeful thoughts boiled through me, I saw the sin of them. Jesus Christ had died for this man; was I going to ask for more? 'Lord Jesus,' I prayed, 'forgive me and help me to forgive him.'

"I tried to smile, I struggled to raise my hand. I could not. I felt nothing, not the slightest spark of warmth or charity. And so again I breathed a silent prayer. 'Jesus, I cannot forgive him. Give me Your forgiveness.'

"As I took his hand the most incredible thing happened. From my shoulder along my arm and through my hand a current seemed to pass from me to him, while into my heart sprang a love for this stranger that almost overwhelmed me.

"And so I discovered that it is not on our forgiveness any more than on our goodness that the world's healing hinges, but on His. When He tells us to love our enemies, He gives, along with the command, the love itself." [2]

To forgive does not mean to atone for that which was done to you. It does not mean that the other person was right and will not be held accountable. Rather, it is a legal action of releasing the debtor from his debt. By forgiving, you are letting that person go free in your heart and leaving them in the hands of a merciful, yet just God. Forgiving others who have wronged us, then, is a legal transaction, just as it was for Jesus to forgive us.

According to the law of God, we were at enmity with Him, guilty and doomed to die. Jesus intervened and took our place, accepting our punishment Himself and allowing us to go free. We have been released from the ultimate debt to a perfect God, and all He asks is that we follow suit in our dealings with others.

This weapon of forgiveness is one that no foe can stand against. When we wield it in obedience to God, the plans of the enemy to crush and bind us are thwarted with one blow. Against forgiveness he has no defense, for it acts as a diffuser of the bomb of hatred he tries to set off. It is, in fact, a gift offered by a loving Father to release freedom and cleansing into our wound. Lewis B. Smedes has written, "When we forgive we set a prisoner free and discover that the prisoner we set free was us." [3]

If we are to be released as warrior women in the army of God, the wound between men and women must be addressed. If you know you carry bitterness and anger toward men, ask the Holy Spirit to help you take steps toward forgiveness. He will lead you through the valley of pain so that you can come out whole on the other side. You may need help in this, so ask Him to bring people into your life whom you can trust and with whom you can share your struggles. There may be some of you who have never told anyone about the abuse inflicted upon you, and it continues to haunt you in the dark and lonely places of your soul. Jesus wants to release you and bring you out into perfect freedom.

Feminism dealt with the issue of women's rights, but in some expressions became infected with the unforgiving wound. God does not want us to emasculate or crush men in order to be released ourselves. Control, manipulation, and demanding to be recognized are the ways of the flesh and will only lead to more strife. As God calls us to rise up in different areas of society, let our hearts be clothed with the cloak of humility, and let us wield the sword of forgiveness.

We are part of the body of Christ, and it would be foolish of us to begin to attack the other half in an effort to move ourselves forward. Let us not presume to take our own place by force, but, rather, let us trust that the Lord will go ahead of us, preparing the place He intends for us to have. As James taught:

Humble yourselves before the Lord, and he will lift you up. James 4:10

We need an invitation from men to enter into the battle beside them. As we noted earlier, Deborah had not planned to go out to war, but Barak invited her to the battle. Let us pray that God will raise up men with the heart of Barak in this hour, men who will recognize that we, men and women alike, are called to fight together.

I believe that the heart of every woman in the church cries out to be looked upon as an equal partner in the kingdom. We may have different tasks and roles, but we know that in Christ there is neither male, nor female. In the Spirit, we all stand as equals in the eyes of God:

You are all sons of God through faith in Christ Jesus, for all of you who were baptized into Christ have clothed yourselves with Christ. There is neither Jew nor Greek, slave nor free, male nor female, for you are all one in Christ Jesus. Galatians 3:26-28

For the men who may be reading this, we women do not want to take over; we just want to be included in the battle for the Lord. We have gifts and strengths that can complement yours. Will you give us an invitation to enter in and join you in the battle?

It would be naïve to believe that the healing between men and women in the church will be accomplished overnight or without a struggle. The wound has penetrated deeply into the body of Christ and left scars. However, it is Christ's body, and His wounds will provide the healing we need. If men and women alike take humble, yet determined steps toward forgiveness and reconciliation, our Lord will meet us in the middle and provide the bridge for us to step across and receive one another in freedom and acceptance. Then we can stand as united warriors, facing our true enemy, assured that complete victory awaits us.

Warrior Women, Arise!

Chapter 7

THE BATTLE
IS NOT AGAINST WOMEN

I DON'T KNOW ABOUT YOU, BUT INTERACTING with other women has not always been easy for me. As a child, I hated the cliques formed at school and abhorred the way one was judged according to dress and style. I always felt as if I was one step behind in trying to keep up with the unspoken rules of the "in" crowd. Young girls can be mercilessly cruel toward each other, using bullying, backbiting, and scorn to wound and control one another. Then, as girls mature into women, this behavior often continues, except that older women find more subtle ways to do it.

What is it with us women? We can be the greatest of friends and support and joy for each other, but we can also compare, idolize, gossip against, and envy each other? How often it happens that, when another woman walks into the room, she is instantly appraised by her weight, beauty, clothes, style, and talent? Those women around her desperately try to find some faults, in order to determine whether or not she is a threat to them. Each one seems to be asking herself, "Is she more beautiful, gifted, or slim than I am?" They may go on to have a conversation with her, which, to the onlooker, appears warm and friendly, but there is often an underlying communication taking place at the same time. The newcomer can be belittled, rejected, or controlled, without a single word being uttered.

Perhaps some of you are protesting, saying that maybe this is true in the world, but surely not in the church. It's time for us to get honest and stop pretending. Many times the very same attitude exists in the church. We're just better at disguising it.

Shall I speak in spiritual terms instead? Our thoughts may go something like this: a woman enters a prayer meeting, and the other women present start to determine how spiritual she is. The following questions may pass through their minds: *How well does she know her Bible? What are her particular gifts? How close is she to God? Is she a threat to my position?* If we feel that she is superior to us in some way—whether in looks or gifts—it causes us to feel inferior, and, therefore, we want to reject and punish her.

Okay, I know that not all of us are like this, but this kind of interaction certainly does happen, and it spreads like poison within God's camp.

Why do we do this? Why does this attitude exist? I would suggest that it is rooted in rejection, insecurity, pride, and a lack of understanding of our Father God's love for each of us. Maybe our earthly fathers never told us we were their beautiful princesses. Maybe we were teased at school or have suffered years of bombardment from the media, and so we believe that we are not beautiful or talented enough to make the mark. Whatever the reasons, we do not feel safe and secure. Therefore, we feel the need to fight others, with comparison and gossip, in order to maintain our position, even though it may be a shaky one.

Girls, the Father has invited us into His kingdom. He has loved us *"with an everlasting love"* (Jeremiah 31:3). With one glance of our eyes, we have captivated His heart (see Song of Songs 4:9), He rejoices over us with singing (see Zephaniah 3:17), He sent Jesus just for us, and nothing can ever separate us from His love (see Romans 8:39).

There are many promises put forth in God's Word regarding His eternal, passionate love for us. Therefore, I believe that God truly wants His daughters to come boldly before His throne of grace in this hour to find grace to help in their time of need (see Hebrews 4:16, KJV). The time for crawling on the floor, hardly believing that He wants to see us, is over. Father God wants to pour out such a revelation of His love on His daughters that we can truly run boldly toward His throne of grace and jump right into His lap.

When we receive the revelation and experience of the Father's passionate love for us, we will be released from wanting to compare ourselves with others. Instead, we can repent of these attitudes and embrace one another in our differences. Consequently, other women need no longer be a threat to us. They are, rather, fellow princesses, allies in the war in which we find ourselves.

We need to be reprogrammed in our thinking in this area, and that will take time. We know that our enemy will not give up easily. He has been planning and scheming his strategy to divide women for centuries. He knows and dreads the power that will be released when we stand together as a united force. When we are tempted to judge and compare, let the fear of the Lord be released over us. We cannot afford to treat each other like this, and I believe it grieves the heart of the Father when we do so. Jealousies and strife have no place in God's body. If you feel the Lord shining His searchlight on this area of your life, repent, turn around, and call out to Him, asking for His forgiveness.

In Joel's prophecy about an army in which there is no competition and where each warrior takes his or her place in perfect harmony, he says: *"They all march in line, not swerving from their course. They do not jostle each other"* (Joel 2:7-8). Women of God, let us become this army, embracing one another and freeing each other to serve in the places to which we have been assigned.

It is vital to remind ourselves of the healing and strengthening power a friendship between two women or girls can be. The Lord has always blessed me with wonderful friendships, which have empowered and encouraged me. As a newborn believer at university, I was surrounded with some precious girls who had grown up in Christian homes. I was desperately in need of their help, as I was a very proud and wounded girl. They discipled, prayed for, laughed with, and, at times, corrected me.

I remember one occasion when I was struggling with ex-boyfriend issues. I had broken up with a guy just before I met Jesus, but we still had strong feelings for each other. Whenever I felt lonely or sad, I would call him, and, at times we would fall back into our relationship. I knew deep inside that it was wrong, but willpower and the fear of God were lacking in me. I was accustomed to going to a person to meet my emotional needs.

One afternoon a new Christian friend of mine called just before my ex was to arrive. She told me that she had felt led to call me just then and give me a verse from the Bible. It was 1 Kings 18:21:

"How long will you waver between two opinions? If the LORD is God, follow him; but if Baal is God, follow him."

In that moment, the fear of the Lord fell on me, and I knew that that this season of double-mindedness in my walk with God was over. It was time to make a firm decision. I asked God for forgiveness and told my boyfriend that I could never see him again. It was one of the defining and life-changing moments in my life. Thank God for a woman who didn't judge or reject me but, rather, in love corrected and encouraged me in my battle against sin and temptation. May God give us His heart toward our sisters who may be caught in sin and inspire us to help them, as my friend did me.

On another occasion, some ten years later, I was an exhausted mother of three, the youngest just a few months old, the oldest five. My husband and I were leading a house church, and I was weary from the battle, worn out both physically and spiritually. In my pride, I had been fighting far too long in my own strength and had come to the point where I was even tempted to take my own life. One Sunday afternoon I was out walking with my baby in the stroller (pram), and it felt as if the hordes of hell were surrounding me. My thoughts and emotions were infiltrated with hopelessness. I knew I could not stand alone, and that this was a deciding point in my life. I called a close friend, who knew how I had struggled during the previous weeks. I confessed to her the state I was in and asked her to stand with me against the enemy and the suicidal thoughts I was having. We prayed, and the power of love and agreement broke through, and I sensed a release.

The hold of the enemy over me that day was broken. I chose to live, and the evil had to flee. I won't claim that life was automatically easy after that, as I still had a journey to take toward total healing and freedom, but I am convinced that the power of that friendship saved my life that day—literally.

We should never underestimate the power of friendship between two women, especially in these difficult times into which we are entering. Fighting alone is no longer an option for us:

Two are better than one,
because they have a good return for their work:

THE BATTLE IS NOT AGAINST WOMEN

If one falls down,
his friend can help him up.
Though one may be overpowered,
two can defend themselves.

Ecclesiastes 4:9-10 and 12

I am now a member of a women's prayer group, and, without my fellow women warriors, would not be writing this book. They pray with me, weep with me when I'm hurting, and fight with me when I'm under attack. When I am uncovered and defeated, they cover my back and remind me of God's promises.

We are of various ages and have different careers and giftings, but when we come together in prayer, we are a mighty group. Each one of us functions in her own anointing and strength, but we complement each other and help one another to stay close to Jesus.

If God has given you good female friendships, thank Him for them, pray protection over them, and steward them well. If you feel alone and don't have anyone to trust right now, ask the Lord for such a friend. He wants us to be connected.

My prayer for all of you reading this book is that you will discover how valuable and precious you are to our heavenly Father and then see the value and beauty in other women around you as well. They are your companions and not your competitors!

Warrior Women, Arise!

Chapter 8

THE BATTLE FOR IDENTITY: OUR APPEARANCE

Stand firm then, with the belt of truth buckled round your waist, with the breastplate of righteousness in place. Take the helmet of salvation.   Ephesians 6:14 and 17

A NUMBER OF YEARS AGO THE MUSICAL ARTIST Prince released a song entitled "The Most Beautiful Girl in the World." The chorus to the song goes like this:

> *Could u be the most beautiful girl in the world?*
> *Could u be?*
> *Its plain 2 see ure the reason that God made a girl.*
> *Oh, yes u are.*

There is something about that song that grabs hold of me every time I hear it. It is as if I am hearing the voice of the Lord Jesus singing those words to me, and in that moment I know that I know that I am totally beautiful and loved. The strange thing is that the result of this is not my turning inward in a narcissistic self-focus, but rather, I find myself singing it right back to the Lord:

Could You be the most beautiful God in the world?

Worship and praise come out of being affirmed in my womanhood. I believe that the words of the song echo the heart of the Father whenever He looks down at His girls. In His eyes, each one of us is the most beautiful girl in the world, and we are the reason He made a girl.

If she is honest, every woman longs to be seen as the most beautiful girl in the world. We long to be admired, wanted, and loved. This is a desire the ultimate Bridegroom, Jesus, has placed inside of us, and only He can ever fully meet that need. God's eyes are ever turned toward us, and He is totally captivated by our beauty.

I wonder if Prince's song touches me so much because it carries something of the spirit of Song of Songs? This Bible book is packed with references to the Bridegroom affirming the beauty of His future bride. One of the early proclamations the Lover makes to His beloved is this:

How beautiful you are, my darling!
  Oh, how beautiful!   Song of Songs 1:15

He repeats this proclamation on three more occasions, and most of what He says is affirming various physical aspects of His bride. He is obviously totally captivated by her beauty and has eyes only for her:

Sixty queens there may be,
and eighty concubines,
and virgins beyond number;
but my dove, my perfect one is unique.

Song of Songs 6:8-9

Our Bridegroom wants to liberate and affirm us in our womanhood, so that we can be the embodiment of His nature on this earth. This knowledge will bring confidence and set us free from all insecurity and poor self-image.

We know that God created both man and woman in His image, and therefore, as women, we reflect an expression of God that is not found in man. The joy of the Lord was expressed on the day that He created woman, as He declared that *"It was very good"* (Genesis 1:31). Up to this point, God had only said that *"it was good"* (Verses 4, 10, 12, 18, 21, and 25), but somehow, after woman entered the world, all was complete, and the ultimate pleasure and satisfaction of the Creator was expressed.

God's pleasure in us is not based solely on our outward appearance. As we know, *"man looks at the outward appearance, but the LORD looks at the heart"* (1 Samuel 16:7). Our Lord is captivated by both our inner and outer beauty.

Peter addressed this issue when he stated:

Your beauty should not come from outward adornment, such as braided hair and the wearing of gold jewelry and fine clothes. Instead, it should be that of

89

your inner self, the unfading beauty of a gentle and quiet spirit, which is of great worth in God's sight.

1 Peter 3:3-4

The core of the message is that our beauty is not dependent upon earthly, external aids, but rather, it shines from within. The issue is not that we can't wear pretty clothes or jewelry, but that we should not rely on these to determine our value and worth. A woman who trusts her God, with a spirit that is unwavering in the face of circumstances, radiates an essence which comes from the throne of God and far outweighs any human beauty. To the degree that we are saturated with Jesus, we will be God's "most beautiful girl in the world."

Understanding just how beautiful we are to the Lord is part of the warrior woman's armor. Armor protects the one involved in warfare and enables them to stand boldly on any battlefield. We must win this battle for beauty so that we can fight as secure and breathtakingly beautiful warriors.

Paul tells us that we are to put on the armor of God, and he gives us the reason:

... so that when the day of evil comes, you may be able to stand your ground, and after you have done everything, to stand. Ephesians 6:13

The mere act of standing is warfare in itself and implies that one of the major tactics of the enemy is to cause us to fall or lose our balance. A warrior may have all the armor, anointing, and gifting available, yet if they cannot stand in battle, they are of little or no use.

We stand as warrior women of God when we know who we are, with the belt of truth firmly buckled around our waist. A woman who knows she is chosen, loved, accepted, called, protected, and equipped can stand in the face of the enemy. We can fight against our foe with fearless abandon, secure in the undying love of our Master for us. Then, when the father of lies shoots his arrows at us, they will have no place to land. Truth is, therefore, one of our greatest weapons—truth about our identity and about God's heart toward us.

In the Western culture that many of us find ourselves immersed in, there is often an attempt to define who we are by external factors—what we look like or do, and our culture, gender, or nationality. For us, as women living in this twenty-first century, the battle for our identity is fierce, and it centers on our appearance.

The bombardment from the media and the entertainment world starts at an early age, attempting to brainwash young girls. Never before has the message been so intense and yet so contradictory. On the one hand, we are programmed to believe that who we are is very much determined by our outward appearance. The underlying message to women is that we are to be slim, beautiful, with perfect complexions, and have wonderfully toned athletic bodies, designer wardrobes, and perfect makeup to match. At the same time, we are conditioned to believe that our value is determined by what we accomplish or do. We should be independent, intelligent, educated women, who can confidently and effortlessly pursue a successful career in which we not only compete with men but, preferably, beat them at their own game. To complete this delicate mixture, we may, of course, have a handsome husband and a home with exquisite interior design, and, if we please, a number of well-adjusted, well-behaved children. The goal is set up; all we have to do is shoot and score.

Unfortunately, the majority of us don't even know how to play this game, let alone win. The one thousandth percent of the female population who do know how to play the game do so with ease, with a little help, of course, from a housekeeper, cook, live-in nanny, gardener, chauffeur, beautician, stylist, interior designer, business advisor, personal trainer, plastic surgeon, and, to top it all off, a therapist! Not surprisingly, the rest of the female population walk around exhausted and with a nagging feeling of failure.

What about women in the Christian world? The messages are pretty much the same, except that religion throws in the extra pressure of wanting to define us by our spiritual performance. We are told to be dedicated, submissive wives, employees, and daughters, who gladly serve others at all times, with a gentle, loving attitude. We should have a fully functioning prayer life in which we pray for our families, cities, nations, and, preferably, world peace too. While none of these things, in themselves, need be wrong, when they are placed onto women as a requirement for acceptance, rather than a consequence of intimacy with God, the result can be suffocating. The stage is set for the perfect woman to arise, except that most of the time she falls flat on her face in despair.

For too long we have passively taken in these messages and allowed our identity, worth, and well-being to be determined by a set of external expectations, destined to crush and smother us. No doubt the enemy, along with our fallen nature, is the mastermind behind this oppressive picture. As long as he can keep us indoctrinated by these expectations, he can control us like puppets on a string. If he wants to hurt us, he need only whisper, "You are fat, ugly, stupid, and not loving enough," and he has us caught in his web for that day.

How many of you recognize this trick? You wake up in the morning, look at your body, see some cellulite appearing, and feel ugly. You watch a movie in which the heroine is everything you feel you are not, and you fall asleep in a fitful state of self-doubt or even self-hate. Dr. Sussie Orbach (psychotherapist, London School of Economics) has discovered that spending just three minutes looking at fashion magazines lowers the self-esteem of eighty percent of women. In a global questionnaire, for which more than three thousand two hundred women from ten different countries were interviewed, two thirds of them agreed that it is a struggle to feel beautiful when confronted with today's beauty ideals.

I don't think many of us need to hear these figures to confirm the reality that we often struggle with. Satan has infiltrated the media to try to dictate to us what beauty is, an image so far removed from reality that it leaves most of us feeling terribly inferior and worthless. If ever there was a battle for us to fight, it is this one—the battle for our beauty. We are not what the media say we must be. We are not what the enemy wants us to be, nor what religious mindsets try to bring us into conformity with. We are who God says we are, the apple of His eye, His beloved, His bride, His children, heirs to His kingdom and promises.

We are in this battle, whether we like it or not, and whether we recognize it or not. I believe it is time for us to rise up, as women, and fight. We need to infiltrate the media and society, letting the One who created women have His say about His intention for them everywhere. We must win this battle, not only for our own sake, but also for coming generations.

Who will protect the young girls of this age? Anorexia, bulimia, suicide, anxiety, panic attacks, and phobias of every kind are all increasing at an alarming rate among young girls. In America alone, there are estimated to be more than ten million women suffering from anorexia and another twenty-five million dealing with a form of binge eating disorder. Recent estimates place the female population at one hundred and fifty million, meaning that a little less than a quarter of women are struggling with serious eating disorders.

Will we stand by and let precious girls be misled, torn, and abused? They desperately need adults who will talk to them, providing role models they can look up to and learn from. We cannot be the blind leading the blind, so first we need to deal with these issues in our own lives. Then we can help others.

The lie that our identity and value rest in how we look is particularly evil and destructive for the younger generation. In Australia, the company producing Dove beauty products has started the Dove Selfesteem Fund. The goal of this fund is to address and counteract messages being sown into the minds of girls and women through the beauty industry. In one of their most famous contributions, Dove executives released a sixty-second film clip in which we see the transformation of a relatively plain-looking woman, through layers of makeup, hair styling, and computer retouching, into a perfect, flawless image placed on a billboard. The woman is transformed almost beyond recognition. The clip ends with these words: "No wonder our perception of beauty is distorted." [1] In fact, almost all the images that we see on billboards or in magazines these days have been retouched using computer effects. These ideals produce low self-esteem in many girls and women and cause them to diet unnecessarily.

I remember my intense struggle as a sixteen-year-old with these issues. I was never officially diagnosed with anorexia nervosa, but I had the symptoms and was well on my way to starving myself to death. My family and I had moved from South Africa to England two years before, and I was still trying to work out who I was and adjust to the new culture and its rules. I started at a boarding school, and in the first week decided that in order to be someone special and likable, I would become thin. I was by no means overweight at the time, but the message had already been implanted in me that I needed to be thinner. I believed that thin was beautiful, thin was acceptable, thin was popular, thin was lovable.

Over the next few months, I proceeded to starve myself. It was not purposefully at first, but gradually my thoughts and my actions became obsessed with food and how I looked. I would look at myself in the mirror and self-hate would grow. The thinner I became, the more I despised and punished myself. I was caught in a sinister trap, whereby, in order to make myself lovable and beautiful, I began to deform and damage my own body. What began as an earnest desire to be beautiful turned into a sinister and deadly game, in which I was the loser.

I would have continued down this path if my parents had not threatened to put me into a hospital. I forced myself to eat more, but the issues of the heart were not dealt with. Within a few months, I fell into bulimia. I would eat vast quantities of food, and then be so overcome with guilt and fear of becoming fat that I would force myself to throw it all up again.

I was caught in another trap, this one full of shame and self-disgust. I was so afraid that someone would discover my awful secret, and, at the same time, I was crying out for help and acceptance. Because I did not know who I was, I allowed lies and media messages about women to determine how I should look and behave.

My journey out of my destructive relationship with food and, ultimately, with myself has been a long and painful one. When I came to know Jesus, at the age of twenty, my behavior changed, but my thought patterns did not. Over the ensuing years I would find myself falling into old habits and, at times, even overeating and throwing up. I would beg God to forgive me because I hated my behavior, but real change came only when He began to replace the enemy's lies with His truth.

It didn't matter how many times my husband or others would say that I was beautiful and not fat; deep down I did not believe them. God had to take me to the very root of my belief system and experience and speak truth to me. Then and only then was I set free, and consequently, my behavior changed. I had to see that my identity was not based on my outward appearance but on my being a daughter of God. I also had to see my actions for what they were and repent of them.

God showed me the pride behind my thoughts. I was placing judgment upon myself and others according to my beliefs, but these were in direct opposition to God's thoughts. I believed I was not worthy of love if my body wasn't a certain way, but God was saying that I was worthy of love because He made me worthy. I was actually rising up in pride and self-will, calling God a liar. If He says I am *"fearfully and wonderfully made"* (Psalm 139:14), who am I to argue with my Maker?

He also showed me how much it hurts Him when I refuse to love my body and take care of it. Again, God has had to reach into the very depths of my being and replace lies with His truth. Slowly I came to see that I am loved and special because He says I am, not because of how I look or feel.

I am far from the person I was when I was sixteen, yet there are days when I still judge myself according to my looks and weight. At such times, I know that I need to allow the Father to saturate me even more with truth so that I can resist these thoughts.

There are so many women, both young and old, who are caught in this trap today. Perhaps not all of them are practicing anorexics or bulimics, but the basic elements are there. I would even venture to say that there are few women in the Western world who are not, in some way, affected in their relationship to food, weight, and their looks. Perhaps you recognize these things in your life or in the lives of those around you.

Women of God, this is an area in which we must fight and win. As women, we represent the beauty and glory of God. Therefore, we should allow Him to shine through us. If we have chosen to live for Jesus, then we are His temple. Our bodies are the chosen dwelling place of the living God. We must allow God to transform our minds so that we will love, nurture, and protect our bodies, treating them with the respect and honor a temple of God deserves.

Let us pray that we will receive an eternal perspective in this area. The bodies we have now are only temporary and will one day be replaced with eternal, perfected ones. The enemy is trying to feed us a gospel that we can have perfect bodies here on earth. The use of Botox and plastic surgery to change our looks and halt the aging process is becoming increasingly popular, but these represent a perversion of our true inheritance. We will be transformed. Our natural bodies are just an external wineskin, mere jars of clay (see 2 Corinthians 4:7).

The world has exalted the outward body and especially that of youth to such a degree that they have become gods and idols in our lives. As women, we have been successfully caught in this trap, and we sin in this regard. This evil has even seeped its way into the church. In Proverbs, the issue of beauty is addressed:

Charm is deceptive, and beauty is fleeting;
  but a woman who fears the LORD is to be praised.
                                          Proverbs 31:30

Our physical bodies will deteriorate, but we can increase in love for our Lord and, consequently, glow.

Who says that old is ugly and young is beautiful? I know an eighty-year-old woman whose face is full of the lines of age. Each line is like an invitation into the mystery and history of her life. She may look old, but she radiates such grace, honor, and regality—more than any fashion model the media have ever presented. She is someone who truly fears the Lord, and her decades of faithfully following and serving Him are expressed in her appearance, making her one of the most beautiful women I have ever met.

For those of you who are struggling with the aging process in your body, remember that your best years are yet to come. Allow all your wisdom, tears, and joy to be released, and shine as the glorious representatives of God that you are. Let us have a healthy respect for our bodies, but, all the same, never forget that they will perish in but a few years.

I remember one of the poignant statements God spoke to me in my journey toward recovery in this area. I was looking at myself in the mirror one evening when I clearly heard the Holy Spirit saying, "Amanda, do you know how much time you waste worrying about your body when soon I will give you a completely new one, which will be yours for eternity?" These words became like electricity shooting through me, and I saw clearly what a ridiculous trap it was:

Therefore we do not lose heart. Though outwardly we are wasting away, yet inwardly we are being renewed day by day. For our light and momentary troubles are achieving for us an eternal glory that far outweighs them all. So we fix our eyes not on what is seen, but on what is unseen. For what is seen is temporary, but what is unseen is eternal. 2 Corinthians 4:16-18

God wants us to take care of our bodies and to steward them well, but understanding that they are only provisional keeps us balanced. In a world so obsessed with the outward appearance, we would be wise to guard our eternal perspective and to place a guard over our hearts, minds, and eyes. Let us be aware of what we watch and listen to. In this area, we can take Paul's exhortation to heart:

Therefore, I urge you, brothers [and sisters], *in view of God's mercy, to offer your bodies as living sacrifices, holy and pleasing to God—this is your spiritual act of worship. Do not conform any longer to the pattern of this world, but be transformed by the renewing of your mind.*   Romans 12:1-2

Precious women, each one of you represents the beauty of God as no one else can. He created and knit you together in your mother's womb, and you are His perfect princess. Embrace His truth about you today, and seek help if you need it. Allow Him to overshadow you with His passionate love and remove the veil over your heart and mind. Jesus is the Lover who battles for you, and no one may call His beloved anything but beautiful.

In another of the Dove advertisements, we see a young boy calling for a girl named Amy outside of her house. She never appears; we just know that she's inside. We see the boy waiting for her and looking dejected, when the following words appear on the screen, "Amy can name 12 things wrong with her appearance … . He can't name one." [2] How true this scenario is for us at times. Jesus comes searching for us, and we are in hiding, focusing on all that we think is wrong with us, believing that these things disqualify us from letting Him in. And all the time He looks upon us with longing and cries out:

All beautiful you are, my darling;
*   there is no flaw in you.*   Song of Songs 4:7

Our Lord is calling to us, His warrior princesses, to come out of our tower of lies and open the door to Him so that He may come in and feast with us. Will you dare to open your heart to Him today? Take His hand and embark on a journey to become a warrior bride. Hear His call:

> *"Arise, my darling,*
>   *my beautiful one, and come with me."*
>
> Song of Songs 2:10

Warrior Women, Arise!

Chapter 9

THE BATTLE FOR IDENTITY: OUR PURPOSE

You may have been verbally or physically abused as a child. You may have been told that you are worthless and that you could never amount to anything. Never believe any person or group or system that negates your individual person. They are not true. Reject their influences. Refuse their doctrines. Shut out their voices. Reject their dogmas, their scrutiny, their assessments.

The only influence that can ever really put you down is your attitude. It can only happen to you through your own choice to listen and to give credit to someone who demoralizes you. Turn them off. Shut them out, and walk into your wonderful, positive world.

You are created in God's image; you have tremendous value. He paid a big price for you. He determined your worth by giving His best, His only Son to redeem you and restore you to Himself as His friend and partner. Does that tell you anything about your value?

— Daisy Washbourne Osborn [1]

DURING THE CHRISTMAS BREAK LAST YEAR, I was talking to God about this book. I hadn't written anything for a few weeks, due to travel, kids with chicken pox, and school holidays, and I was beginning to feel more like a worn-out Martha than a victorious Deborah. I began to be fearful and wondered if I really could accomplish this task. I was asking myself why God had chosen me. Was I really the best person for the job? I was focusing on all my inadequacies and weaknesses and had become discouraged.

By the ocean at the time, I looked out at the vast expanse of water and saw the greatness and beauty of the Lord in nature, and it suddenly hit me that my only qualification for writing the book was that my heavenly Father had told me to do it. His will was the beginning and end of my qualifications. I could focus on my inabilities or lack of worth until I was blue in the face, but it would never make any difference.

The tasks God assigns us are not based on our own ability and endeavor, but on His will. If He tells us to do something for Him, then we know He will give us the ability and strength to complete it. How freeing to know that whatever we accomplish here on earth for Jesus is not based on human achievement, but on the calling of God and His will for us. When we understand this, then whatever He calls us to do, we can be one hundred percent confident that we can do it, as we believe His promises:

The one who calls you is faithful and he will do it.
1 Thessalonians 5:24

THE BATTLE FOR IDENTITY: OUR PURPOSE

I can do all things through Christ who strengthens me. Philippians 4:13, NKJV

No longer do we have to be bound to the yo-yo of our emotions, dependent upon how holy or perfect we feel or act each day. Externals do not determine who or what we are; God's love does. This protects us from a religious performance mentality by which we try to compete with each other in order to establish our position and then run around in a frenzy of activity, trying to earn God's approval.

How many of you have ever asked yourself, "What am I doing with my life?" or thought "I don't seem to be accomplishing anything of lasting worth"? In a world where we are often fed the lie that our worth is determined by what we do, it is easy to start asking ourselves these kinds of questions. But if we are to stand in warfare, as Paul admonishes us to, then this deception regarding our identity needs to be dismantled.

The concept of performance-based worth is particularly strong in the Western world, where career and achievements are elevated to an alarming height. Children learn at an early age that their performance in school, sports, music, and art is what defines them. As they grow and develop, cords of this sinister concept become so intertwined with their thought processes that by the time they reach adulthood, the unspoken rule is that it's not who you *are*, but what you *do* that counts.

Our profession or gifting can help to define us and give an indication of the kind of person God has made us, but when it becomes the only factor, it can be very destructive. God's kingdom is in direct contradiction to this. In His kingdom, we cannot earn our place; it is a gift:

> *For it is by grace you have been saved, through faith—and this not from yourselves, it is the gift of God—not by works, so that no one can boast.* Ephesians 2:8-9

God calls us His righteous children, inheritors of eternal life, and He shares His power and Spirit with us as we simply put our faith in Him. When we decide to follow Him, these things are available to us even before we accomplish anything at all for Him. We can never earn His love, nor perform our way into His acceptance. All of our outward attributes—looks, abilities, gifts, careers, even sacrifices—can never affect our identity as a child of God. Part of the armor that God has given us is the breastplate of righteousness, which protects our heart, and another is the helmet of salvation, which covers our head, or mind.

Kathryn Kuhlman could fill whole stadiums wherever she traveled. People would stand in line for hours in order to be assured of a place in her meetings. The sick and needy would travel thousands of miles in the hope of receiving healing. The expectations on her and her meetings were enormous, yet this petite woman had no illusions that she could give her public anything in her own strength. While speaking to a large audience, she once said, "You want to know the why of these miracles? ... It is not Kathryn Kuhlman, it's not some personality ... .

These great crowds come not because of Kathryn Kuhlman. I wouldn't walk across the street to see her. I have news for you, she's the most ordinary person you've ever seen in your life.

"I die a thousand deaths before I walk out onto a platform. I don't care where it is, I don't care how large or small the auditorium or how large the size of the crowd. I die a thousand deaths. I die a thousand deaths because I know better than anyone else in the whole world that I cannot give it to you, that I have no healing virtue, I have no healing power. You and I are dependent on the power of the Holy Spirit." [2]

This woman understood that she had nothing in herself to give to her God or to others but that it was her reliance on the Holy Spirit and agreement with what He said about her that allowed miracles to flow freely from her life. If we are to become warriors for Jesus, we must have this same foundation.

Jesus is our new identity. The old is gone, and the new has come. Now our identity is not based on our family, nationality, gender, gifting, or even our failures, but on the character of God Himself. He wants to live through us. When we accept Jesus into our lives, the breastplate of righteousness is a gift given to us by the Lord. It is nothing we can earn ourselves. May God give us the Spirit of wisdom and revelation so that we can understand these facts.

When true spiritual identity is formed in us, we will automatically be transformed in our everyday life, in our actions, our feelings, and even our thoughts. If we are to be able to fight victoriously for Him, we each need to allow our Lord to take us on this journey. How can we stand against unrighteousness in the world around us and preach God's Good News if we don't believe He has made us righteous and that we have authority based on His Word and not on our abilities or lack thereof? Jesus told His disciples:

> *"I am the vine; you are the branches. If a man remains in me and I in him, he will bear much fruit; apart from me you can do nothing."*   John 15:5

What was Jesus really trying to say to us in this passage? Many of us interpret this to mean that we can do nothing except _____ , and here we add our own little list of tasks we think we can or should do without Him. But no! When Jesus says *"nothing"* He means "nothing"! We cannot even breathe without Him, because He is the One who created our lungs and who also keeps the earth's atmosphere in balance so that we have air to breathe. Far too many times God's people have tried to accomplish things for Him in their own human strength.

The story of Martha and Mary (see Luke 10:38-42) speaks poignantly to us, as women, regarding this issue. Martha, like many women in the church today, was a dedicated, hardworking, faithful follower of Jesus. She knew that He was coming to visit, and so she spent her energies on getting things ready for Him. She wanted Him to have good food to eat and a clean and orderly house to sit in when He came. This all seems reasonable enough. Martha wanted to make Jesus feel welcome, to the best of her ability.

Mary, on the other hand, was not even aware of these concerns. As soon as Jesus stepped into their house, she simply sat at His feet and received from Him. When Martha complained to Jesus about Mary's lack of help, to the human mind her complaint seemed perfectly justified. Why should she do all the work? But Jesus saw the situation from an eternal perspective. I believe He recognized Martha's genuine desire to show Him her love through her works for Him. However, it was not her works that He was after; it was her heart. Jesus proclaimed that Mary had chosen the better part, because she simply wanted to be close to Him. The same is true for us today in the 21st century. God wants relationship, not workers:

"You are my friends if you do what I command. I no longer call you servants, because a servant does not know his master's business. Instead, I have called you friends, for everything that I learned from my Father I have made known to you." John 15:14-15

Too often we get caught in the subtle trap of *doing* rather than *being*. We may begin with a genuine desire to serve God, but our efforts end up being done in our own strength, and the result is that we feel tired and resentful. Jesus wants intimacy with us, and anything we accomplish for Him must be a fruit of that.

Therefore, if we hope to be fruitful for our Lord Jesus, we must know Him well. He said:

"Remain in me, and I will remain in you. No branch can bear fruit by itself; it must remain in the vine. Neither can you bear fruit unless you remain in me."

John 15:4

Most of us have read these words and probably heard great sermons preached on them, but how many of us live them out on a daily basis? The message is very simple: a branch cannot grow separated from the vine, for that's where it gets its nourishment and strength. I'm sure that we, at times, must look like a branch cut off from the vine and without a proper source of water, slowly scorching and withering in the sun. In this state, we too often look up toward the vine, wondering how it could have allowed us to be cut off like this.

The enemy hates intimacy. He cannot understand it, but he has seen it. He has seen God's love firsthand. He knows the power of unity, and it frightens him. He will do anything to distort and disguise God's will for us to have this oneness with Him. If the enemy cannot get God's people to be tempted by the world, he will try to get us to do "good" deeds, motivated by human striving and fear.

The gospel that many Christians live and believe today is so distorted and destructive that it must cause the Father much heartache. Most believers start their journey hearing that they are saved by grace, but then they somehow begin to believe that they must earn this grace through living a life dominated by obligations based on others' expectations and judgments. Many of them believe that they must pray, evangelize, read and memorize their Bibles, be loving, faithfully attend church and, preferably, an extra prayer meeting ... all in order to meet the unspoken requirements of an angry and demanding Father, who is ready to punish and judge them at any time if they slack off. No wonder much of the Western church is burned out, angry, hard-hearted, and disillusioned! It is even less of a surprise that the world looking on wants nothing to do with this form of Christianity.

This message is a vile distortion of the Gospel of Christ. Jesus was sent in order to offer us eternity close to our Maker, starting now. We are no longer bound over to a life of darkness and pain. We can be close to our Father and share our everyday life with Him. In fact, He offers us His power and presence in the most mundane areas of our lives and has promised never to leave nor forsake us. We have His power to overcome evil, sin, and sickness. We do not have to wander alone in this broken world, even though trials and suffering may come.

Our hope is not in having a problem-free life here on earth, but our hope is set on our inheritance of an eternity free from pain. Jesus wants to be close to us, and whatever we then do for Him should be a result of this knowledge. If the only thing we could accomplish was to lie in bed all day, this would not affect our identity. There is no external factor that can affect your worth outside of your Father's words. No matter how much or how little you have achieved today, know that in the eyes of the Father you are His precious, beloved daughter.

Let us enter into this battle for identity by embracing the truth about ourselves, and, as we the know the truth, the truth will set us free.

Warrior Women, Arise!

Chapter 10

THE WARRIOR'S SHIELD

IF THE LORD IS TO RAISE US UP AS A MIGHTY ARMY, then we must learn to fight. No one is born a warrior, and one can become a warrior only through years of practice and discipline. According to *The American Heritage Dictionary of the English Language,* a *warrior* is defined as "one who is engaged in or experienced in battle" or "one who is engaged aggressively or energetically in an activity, cause, or conflict."

I watched the movie *The Last Samurai,* the story of Nathan Algren, an American military advisor who embraces the samurai culture he has been sent to destroy. In an early scene, Algren (played by Tom Cruise) finds himself a captive in a samurai village. He picks up a child's wooden sword and, using it, tries to fight against a samurai warrior. Not surprisingly, he is repeatedly beaten and knocked to the ground because he is untrained in this form of warfare. But he continues to pick himself up, determined not be defeated. He has the heart of a warrior, even though he lacks training and skills. Eventually, after months of observing and training with the samurai people, Algren becomes a skilled samurai warrior himself.

What struck me about this movie was that although Nathan Algren did not know how to fight and was constantly being knocked to the ground, he had an unwavering desire to learn, and that desire drove him forward. I thought to myself how very often we are like that. We don't really know how to do battle against our enemy, and many times he knocks us around, leaving us bloodied and wounded on the floor. But each of us has the heart of a warrior downloaded within us. The Spirit of God lives inside of us, and that Spirit burns with a passion and calling for us to develop into overcomers.

It does not matter how many blows or defeats you have experienced in your lifetime; you can be trained to be a mighty warrior for God. This is your inheritance and destiny. All God needs is your willingness to submit to His training, and He can do the rest. He needs men and women who are willing to surrender to Him—their lives, their hearts, their time, and their visions—so that He can turn them into conquerors.

David was a mighty warrior, one who constantly found himself in battle, and yet he understood the need for training in order to fight well. He said:

> *He* [God] *trains my hands for battle;*
> *my arms can bend a bow of bronze.*
> *You give me your shield of victory,*
> *and your right hand sustains me;*
> *you stoop down to make me great.*
>
> Psalm 18:34-35

David began his training as a warrior while tending sheep for his father and learning to defend them against lions and bears. Later, he fought and defeated the Philistine giant Goliath and then went on to perform great feats of bravery as a warrior in King Saul's army. Later in his life, David fought as king himself against the enemies of Israel. Battle will follow us in our journey with God. The nature of it may change, but the principles remain the same.

Sadly, the Church has often missed one of its callings: namely, to be a training place for warriors. Instead, we women have been taught to make coffee, become "nice" people, and sing pretty songs. The consequence of this is that new believers are often never informed of the fact that following Jesus automatically places them in a war zone, and this puts them at serious risk. Jesus is on our side, and He is all-powerful, but we, as His disciples, need to learn how to use well the power He gives us.

One of the weapons our Lord has given us is *"the shield of faith"*:

In addition to all this, take up the shield of faith, with which you can extinguish all the flaming arrows of the evil one.   Ephesians 6:16

In olden times, battles often consisted of close hand-to-hand combat. There were no guns, missiles, or bombs to be fired from long distances. If you were to fight the enemy, you did so in fierce personal combat. This was the kind of combat Paul was implying when he discussed warfare with the Ephesian believers. The word *shield* here means "a large shield or door" and comes from the Greek root word meaning "a portal, or entrance, door, gate." The shield of faith Paul is talking about is the entrance port at which the enemy wishes to come in with his lies. Faith is our protection that determines whether or not we allow those lies (the flaming arrows of the enemy) to come in. With faith, we can extinguish them.

In our everyday lives, the enemy stands before us ready to fight us, and too many times we are not even aware of his presence. His arrows are directed at us, causing us to question the character and faithfulness of God. This battle, then, is about character and trust. The enemy wants to shoot arrows of doubt and mistrust at us, but faith is able to shield us, through the simple act of trusting in God.

In those former days, a shield was vital to defending oneself against arrows and the up-close blows of an opponent. Picture a person standing in front of enemy troops, with arrows hissing at him from every side. Imagine that this person has a shield but allows it to hang at his side. The arrows are falling upon him, and his life is in imminent danger, but he does not even bother to lift his shield in an effort to defend himself.

"That's crazy," you might say. "Who would be so stupid?" Well, sadly, that person who fails to use a shield is often you, and it is often me, when we are faced with the fiery darts of the enemy coming against us today. We don't take up our shield of faith, we don't trust God, and, consequently, we allow those fiery darts to pierce and wound us.

Faith can protect us from being overcome. When darts of unbelief, shame, pride, fear, and temptation come at us, we can simply take up our shield and push them back.

Faith, in this context, means "conviction, reliance upon Christ, persuasion," and comes from the Hebrew root word meaning "to convince, to pacify, to trust, obey, yield." When the enemy throws doubt and adverse circumstances at us, we can defend ourselves through the simple act of trusting that God is with us in that particular situation. We yield our feelings and fears to the Spirit of God and choose to trust and obey His Word.

This sounds easier than it often proves to be for us. Why is it that we don't pick up our shield in certain circumstances? I would suggest some reasons: our lack of awareness of the battle at hand and, at times, our lack of faith or trust in God in that particular situation.

The Scriptures tell us that *"faith comes from hearing ... the word"* (Romans 10:17). God is only too happy to reward us when we truly seek Him. The more we hear and understand God's Word, the stronger our faith becomes and the easier it is for us to trust Him. Faith comes from knowing the Word, Jesus Himself. The more we understand who God is and experience Him in our everyday life, the stronger our faith and, therefore, our ability to use our shield will be.

When I was still a young believer, God told me to go to Colorado Springs, Colorado, to be part of a Youth With A Mission (YWAM) school on intercession and spiritual warfare. I was excited, as I really wanted to go, but there was one minor problem: I had no money and needed more than $2,000.00 to pay the school fees. I sensed the Holy Spirit encouraging me to proceed anyway, despite the concerns of my parents and friends. I had only been a believer for three years, and those who were more mature around me had concerns about my ability to hear God in this situation. In fact, I think many of them felt that I had really "lost it." But one woman, my spiritual mother at the time, encouraged me to follow what I believed in my heart.

To be perfectly honest, I was petrified, and the night before I was to depart for Colorado Springs, I could hardly sleep. The next day, when I was finally seated on the plane and was on my way, my mind was bombarded with fiery darts from the enemy. His words accused me, "What are you doing, you crazy woman? God will never provide for you. They will kick you out of that school, and you'll be stranded there. What makes you think that it was God who told you to go in the first place?" During the entire eight-hour flight, God was silent, while the enemy spoke very loudly, and my heart was a wreck.

When we arrived in Denver, a group of Christians boarded the plane, and one of the men had a Bible verse written on his T-shirt. It said:

"Have I not commanded you? Be strong and courageous. Do not be terrified; do not be discouraged, for the LORD your God will be with you wherever you go."

Joshua 1:9

The words on that shirt spoke directly to my heart, and my shield of faith suddenly was raised, and I was sure that God would be faithful to supply for me.

On arrival at the school, we were expected to pay the school fees. As I stood in line, I still had only a few dollars in my pocket, but I was convinced that an angel would appear to give me the money I lacked. Then, as the line dwindled and I got closer to a confrontation with school officials, my faith also dwindled, and stress and fear again bubbled up inside of me.

When my turn came, there was no angel, no money, and just a lot of fiery darts. I tried to explain my situation and how God was a little late in providing my need. I was told that I could stay that week, but if no money came by that time, then I would have to leave. I left the line that day crushed and found a quiet place where I could vent my feelings to God. I was angry and told Him I thought it had been mean of Him to send a young girl across to the other side of the world and then leave her stranded in this way.

In the midst of my outburst, I heard the Spirit of God saying, "Amanda, you do not know Me or My character, but I am going to teach you to know both." The fear of God fell on me, and I saw my pride and unbelief in this situation. If God says that He is always faithful, then who was I to argue—no matter what the circumstances looked like? I asked His forgiveness, and as I walked back to my room, a girl came up to me and told me that God had spoken to her to pay $100.00 toward my fees! For the next five months, the Lord faithfully provided all the money

I needed, for the school and also for an outreach to India and Israel.

Through that experience my faith was tested, but it also grew, as I saw in action that God's words about His character are true, and the next time I was faced with the challenge of trusting God in the area of finances it was much easier to take up my shield of faith and trust Him. I was able to use my testimony to quench the enemy's darts of unbelief, with the truth that my Daddy God is faithful. If He says He will provide, then He will do it. It's as simple as that. And, with that, all the fiery darts of the wicked one were officially extinguished! This is how we can use our testimony of what God has done for us to overcome the enemy (see Revelation 12:11).

Now that was a great testimony of how God had proved Himself faithful, and looking back, it was easy to see that He is and always has been good, but what about those occasions when everything seems to go wrong? What about the times when we are experiencing great suffering or loss, and the faithfulness of God in action seems far removed from our reality? What do we do when we experience the loss of a child, divorce, broken homes, lost jobs, or when we are facing debt or sickness? How can we hold up the shield of faith then? These are severe tests for all of God's children, and few of us have found the secret of always trusting Him in the face of suffering or trials.

The enemy longs to use our current circumstances to cause us to come into agreement with him. He throws his accusations at us, which might sound like this: "See,

God doesn't really care!" "What kind of loving father would allow that?" "Curse God, for He's left you now!" "See, He has stopped loving you." Satan wants us to doubt God and, therefore, lose hope. But Jesus *"is the same yesterday and today and forever"* (Hebrews 13:8). He cannot change. If He says He is faithful, slow to anger, and abounding in love, and that He will never leave us nor forsake us, then He cannot lie. Circumstances may shout. They may scream, and we may struggle to understand why God allows many things in this world to happen, yet His character remains constant. Faith is simply us coming into agreement with what God says about Himself, no matter what our circumstances happen to be at the moment.

Job was severely tested in this area of trust. When his livestock and then his own sons and daughters were killed, he still worshiped God, proclaiming:

> *"Naked I came from my mother's womb,*
> *and naked I will depart.*
> *The LORD gave and the LORD has taken away;*
> *may the name of the Lord be praised."*   Job 1:21

A few days later. Job found himself covered with painful sores over his entire body, and his wife taunted him, *"Curse God and die."* He answered her with these wise words:

> *"Shall we accept good from God, and not trouble?"*
> Job 2:10

Job chose to trust God, even when all the circumstances around him seemed to bring into question His faithfulness and goodness. In fact, the very reason Job found himself in such a place of suffering in the first place was that the enemy questioned his ability to be a God-fearing man in the face of trial.

The Lord, on the other hand, was convinced that Job would remain true to Him, no matter what the enemy threw at him. It is in the dark, hidden places of trial and suffering that our faith can shine and be our shield. It is in those moments of much desperation and doubt that we can stand among the heroes of faith, by simply choosing to trust that God is there and that He will come to our aid.

Maria Woodworth-Etter, the great American woman evangelist, described her feelings when a fifth child was taken from her by death: "This sad bereavement nearly took my life. The dear Savior was never so near and real to me before. He was by my side and seemed to bear me up in His loving arms. I could say, 'The Lord gave and the Lord has taken away; blessed be the name of the Lord.' "[1]

This woman was given the grace to be able to respond as Job did to suffering. She did not deny the pain she felt, and yet she still chose to trust her Savior—no matter how dreadful the situation. This, I believe, touches the heart of God more than any great miracle or work of service we could ever do for Him. A child looking up to Him, despite not being able to see, feel or hear Him, touches the Father like nothing else can, and He promises that such a person will be blessed:

"Blessed are those who have not seen and yet have believed." John 20:29

This is something Satan cannot understand, for he is so full of pride and self-seeking that he cannot fathom the mystery of love and faith in an unseen God. This is even a mystery for the angels in heaven. They serve and honor God because they are surrounded by His glory day and night. They are compelled to worship Him. We, on the other hand, cannot see and, many times, cannot feel our Creator. We live in a broken world, one full of suffering, disappointments, and many other consequences of the Fall. Still, we have the capacity to worship and love God with all our heart, soul, and mind. Our decision to trust Him raises up a shield of faith to protect us.

Knowing God in our everyday lives and experiencing His faithfulness, in both good and bad times, is a powerful weapon for us to use, and God wants to train and teach us to put up our shield. When we are faced with circumstances in which the darts of the enemy are hitting us, we must realize that there may be holes in our shield that need to be mended. Such holes might have come from wounds we suffered in the past, which the enemy is aware of and which he takes advantage of in order to hurt us.

For example, you may be someone who had a very angry parent, one who could even become physically and/or verbally abusive when provoked. You, therefore, learned as a child that another person's anger is something dangerous and can leave you hurt and vulnerable.

Now, twenty years later, you are in a store, and you accidentally bump into a man in the aisle. He flies into a fit of rage, shouting at you and demanding an apology. You are reminded of your abusive past, and fear of another's anger rises up within you.

In that moment, you may give way to fear, panic, shame, and self-hatred, and for the rest of the day, this event may stay with you, causing you to feel defeated and wounded. The enemy has used this situation to shoot fiery darts at you, and because of your unhealed wounds from the past, your shield of faith is down. You may know (with your mind) that God is with you, but your emotional experience says that when someone else is angry, you can get hurt.

We all have experiences like this; and as we are living in the present, memories from the past can be triggered. We may have all the right theology and Bible verses, but in certain situations, lies from the past manifest themselves. The enemy knows those lies because, more often than not, it was he who implanted them in us through traumatic experiences with others. How, then, do we deal with these situations? Ask God to reveal Himself to you through the circumstance. Let Him speak His truth into your emotions and memories at that moment. God's truth about the matter brings healing, so that the next time you meet an angry person, you can put up a shield and know that the Lion of Judah is there with you and you have nothing to fear. When you do this, the arrows of the enemy will bounce off of your shield, and you will be able to continue your day unharmed.

God is not at all interested in or impressed by our attempts to please Him by fighting on our own. Simple trust and a healthy fear of Him are what He is looking for in His children:

His pleasure is not in the strength of the horse,
nor his delight in the legs of a man;
the LORD delights in those who fear him,
who put their hope in his unfailing love.

Psalm 147:10-11

And without faith it is impossible to please God, because anyone who comes to him must believe that he exists and that he rewards those who earnestly seek him.

Hebrews 11:6

Again, our greatest defense is keeping our hearts soft and trusting toward our Father. Following Jesus places us in a battle, but He has also equipped us, so that we can both attack our enemy and defend ourselves. We have all been given a shield. Let us train to use it daily and, thus, become skillful warriors.

Warrior Women, Arise!

Chapter 11

THE WARRIOR'S SWORD

Take ... the sword of the Spirit, which is the word of God.   Ephesians 6:17

ONLY A FOOL WOULD GO OUT TO FIGHT WITHOUT weapons. They are needed both to go on the attack and to defend oneself against the enemy. If we could see our everyday lives through the eyes of the Spirit, I am convinced that we would see ourselves under constant attack, yet seldom using the weapons we have available to us. How many times have God's people found themselves beaten up, defeated, and left to die on the battlefield? If the One who is in us is greater than the one who is in the world (see 1 John 4:4), then something must be wrong. God has equipped us with everything we need to fight, yet, through lack of training, lack of understanding and unbelief, many times we stand before the enemy without ever taking up our weapons of warfare.

Too often we do not understand our authority in Christ, nor the nature of our enemy. I know this has often been the case in my own life. For years I struggled with the belief that I could not do anything and that I was not really made for this world. These lies were a source of great torment to me and resulted in my becoming paralyzed and not daring to become involved in many activities. I embraced these lies as my identity and even hid behind them, so as not to fail. When I heard the lies whispering to me, I failed to resist them, and I didn't take up my shield of faith or use the sword of the Spirit. I didn't trust my Daddy God, and I paid dearly for it.

When I look back now, I realize that if I had just taken up arms against the enemy in the beginning, his lies would have been deflected, and I would have saved myself years of pain and defeat. When I finally did stand up and fight with the sword of God's truth, I was amazed how swiftly the lies left me.

No warrior woman is complete without her sword. She needs it, both to defend herself and to destroy her enemy. As a warrior, she must learn to know and trust her sword, training to use it daily, even in times of peace. The sword is the warrior's friend and should be taken with her wherever she goes. A warrior who is alert and prepared eats, sleeps, and lives every moment with the sword by her side, ever ready to wield it at the slightest hint of an attack.

As God's warrior women, our sword is His Word, and we need to know it, read it, study it, memorize it, pray it, proclaim it, and sing it until it becomes a part of who we are. We cannot expect to stand and defeat the enemy of our souls if we are not one with the sword we are using. It is important for us to own it and, perhaps most of all, allow it to own us. We come against the enemy, not with the words of man, but with the words of the very

God who created the universe through the utterance of His mouth.

In a recent film adaptation of *Alice in Wonderland,* we see Alice in a new light. She has found herself in Wonderland, which is under the oppressive rule of the Mad Red Queen, whose harshness and tendency to cut off her opponents' heads is terrorizing the people. Not only this, but the queen also has a fearsome dragon, Jabberwocky, under her command. During the course of the film, we watch as Alice boldly recovers a sword which is destined to slay this dragon and returns it to its rightful owner, the White Queen.

In the White Queen's castle, there is a suit of armor waiting to be worn by the one destined to defeat Jabberwocky. As the queen places the reclaimed sword beside the rest of the armor, she states, "The armor is complete; now all we need is a champion." How these words ring true for us as warrior women! God has prepared and equipped us with armor, and with the sword in place, all that is needed is for us to arise as champions, destined to defeat our foe.

You don't have to have years of theological training, and you don't have to know Greek and Hebrew. These can be helpful, but to be able to use the sword, you need to know Him who is the Word—Jesus.

In the book that bears his name, John describes Jesus as the Word of God (see John 1:1-2), and in the book of Revelation, he describes Him in this way:

He is dressed in a robe dipped in blood, and his name is the Word of God.   Revelation 19:13

Jesus is the very embodiment of God's written Word. To know one line of the Bible and be deeply connected with its Author is far more powerful than knowing the words in theory and yet not knowing the One who wrote them. The Word is an invitation into intimacy and relationship. It belongs to you, and it is yours to use to crush the head of the enemy. It may be that you feel inadequate in this whole area and do not feel that you truly know how to use the sword, but God will teach you how to take it up in order to fulfill His purposes.

In a later scene in the same film, Alice discovers that in the prophecies of old, it is she who is destined to end the reign of the Mad Queen by slaying Jabberwocky. This she is to do with the very sword she has recovered from the enemy's camp. Earlier in the film, the idea of being used in any kind of combat is totally foreign to her, and she firmly asserts, "I'm not slaying anything. I don't slay, so put it out of your mind."

Now that Alice has realized that she is, in fact, called to slay, she is afraid and has no idea how she will ever be able to defeat such a dreadful dragon. She shares her concerns with the Blue Caterpillar, who has been a sort of advisor to her in the whole process, and he speaks the following words to her: "The sword knows what it wants. All you need to do is to hold on to it."

Some of you may relate to this. You do not really know how you are to use the sword to defeat the enemy in your life and in the lives of those around you, but, warrior women, God's Word knows what needs to be done in order to overcome the enemy. We need only hold on to it and let it fight through us. God has put it like this:

As the rain and the snow
  come down from heaven,
and do not return to it
  without watering the earth
and making it bud and flourish,
  so that it yields seed for the sower
  and bread for the eater,
so is my word that goes out from my mouth:
  It will not return to me empty,
but will accomplish what I desire
  and achieve the purpose for which I sent it.
                                    Isaiah 55:10-11

You may feel that you are no theologian or expert on the Bible, but that does not mean that you can't be a warrior. The sword belongs to you. It is part of the armor God has given to all His children. We need to understand our royal heritage, as children of the King, and to embrace the sword and live as overcomers. Let us train to use God's Word, seeking purpose when we read it, and asking God's Holy Spirit to unveil its secrets.

Our focus should not be on acquiring head knowledge in order to appear learned, but, rather, earnestly seeking the heart of our Father, asking Him to give us understanding about His truths. If we come with a childlike, humble and teachable spirit, He will reveal to us hidden treasures in His Word. Jesus Himself proclaimed that it gives God great pleasure to reveal His secrets to the childlike (see Matthew 11:25-26).

There is so much about God's Word, the sword, which we have not understood, but in order to be effective warriors, He wants us to diligently seek after these treasures:

> *It is the glory of God to conceal a matter;*
> *to search out a matter is the glory of kings.*
>
> Proverbs 25:2

As we understand our royal heritage (as daughters of the King), reading and knowing His Word will no longer be a burden or something equated with condemnation but, rather, with excitement and adventure.

I don't know how it is for you, but my relationship with the Word of God has not always been clear-cut. When I first came to know Jesus, at the age of twenty, I had very little religious background, but I knew that the Bible was something important and was repeatedly told that I needed to read it daily. At first, however, it had little relevance to or impact on me. I am a very relational type of person, and therefore, in order to be motivated in any area, I need to see a relational connection. The same was true for me and the Word. Words on a piece of paper meant little or nothing to me ... until I began to know the One who had written them and to discover His purpose for them.

At first I was quite confused about many passages in the Bible and would cry out to God to show me what they meant. He began to highlight certain verses and passages that spoke to my situation or need at that moment, and suddenly the words brought life and power to me. In particular, He would show me verses that related to a person who was broken and/or in emotional pain, such as:

The LORD is close to the brokenhearted
and saves those who are crushed in spirit.

Psalm 34:18

As this was my almost constant state at the time, this brought me great comfort and confidence to continue to get to know this God better. I was able to make the connection I needed, and suddenly God's Word applied to my everyday life. I took the truth that my Daddy in heaven loved and accepted me, and used it to stand against the feelings of rejection and worthlessness I struggled with. This truth now became a sword in my hands.

When God's Word is mentioned in the Bible, it is described with one of two Greek words, either *logos* or *rhema*. *Logos* refers to the written Word as a whole, while *rhema* refers to a specific spoken word. We need to know both forms of the Word if we are to fully understand the power of the sword.

In Ephesians 6, when discussing the area of warfare, Paul tells us to take up the Word of God, and in this case, it is the Greek word *rhema* that is used. In order to defeat the enemy in one-on-one combat, we must have God's specific word, or truth, for that situation.

The way in which God will speak to each of us will be different, depending on our personalities and giftings, but each will recognize the voice of the Good Shepherd. It is His still, small voice whispering words of love and truth that we need to learn to know as never before. This will be vital in the days ahead, when, during persecution, we may even be denied access to the Bible.

It is natural that God's Word can speak to each of us in different ways, depending upon our situation or particular need. However, it is important that we seek an understanding of all of His Word, not just parts of it, if we are to be able to use this mighty tool effectively.

Knowing the Word and being trained in hearing it directly is the way in which we sharpen our sword, to stand in the times of great battle ahead. Throughout my nearly twenty years of knowing God, there have been many different periods in my walk with the Bible. There have been seasons in which I would study it and become very engrossed in its revelations, times when I would read it little if at all (especially when my children were small and my time was so limited), and perhaps the majority of the time when I read it purely out of obedience, not always feeling or sensing any great revelation, but choosing to eat of it anyway. It is rather like our need for food; we eat because we know we need it in order to function properly. There may be times of feasting and special treats, but, for the greater part of our lives, eating is just a necessary habit for our survival and well-being. So it is with God's Word. If we do not consume the Word on a regular basis, we will grow weak and powerless.

We all want freedom in our lives, and the way to get that freedom is by knowing Jesus, both through a personal relationship and through His written Word. He said:

> *"If you hold to my teaching, you are really my disciples. Then you will know the truth, and the truth will set you free."*   John 8:31-32

These are not just words or empty promises, but this is our inheritance as God's princesses—total freedom. This freedom is ours to take, and while it may be a process to be worked out in our lives, we are destined to have the testimony of David:

> *"I pursued my enemies and crushed them;*
> * I did not turn back till they were destroyed.*
> *I crushed them completely, and they could not rise;*
> * they fell beneath my feet.*
> *You armed me with strength for battle;*
> * you made my adversaries bow at my feet."*
>   2 Samuel 22:38-40

Sadly, for many of us, the present reality of our lives does not communicate the victorious testimony above. Something is wrong somewhere. God's warriors are not using their sword. What better strategy could any enemy have than to take his opponent's sword and then turn it against him. Well, Satan, our enemy, has been doing this since the very beginning. In the Garden of Eden, he came to the mother of all women, Eve, and took the "word" God had spoken to her and Adam and twisted it, causing her to doubt her Father's love and good will toward her. Satan began to sow doubt and confusion in her mind regarding what God had said:

> *"Did God really say, 'You must not eat from any tree in the garden?' "* Genesis 3:1

Once Satan had sowed the seed of doubt, he then went for the kill, implying that God had been trying to hold something back from His children by not allowing them to eat from the tree of the knowledge of good and evil:

> *"You will not surely die," the serpent said to the woman. "For God knows that when you eat of it your eyes will be opened, and you will be like God, knowing good and evil."* Genesis 3:4-5

Satan tried to place his word as truth over the Word of God, but as the great father of lies, lies are all he could come up with.

Sadly, Eve fell for this deception and chose to believe the accusations against her Creator, rather than trust His word. This strategy of twisting God's original word against a woman and keeping her separated from her God was so very successful that he has continued to use it ever since. Many times Satan twists words, even words from the Bible, to crush and enslave women, causing them to believe that they are inferior beings and not wanted in their Father's kingdom. How many of us have had the Word of God used against us, to keep us bound or hindered from fulfilling our destiny? Many times that Word has been twisted, taken out of context, or imposed through the eyes of sexism, to bind the women of God.

At the time of the Fall, God told Satan:

> *"I will put enmity*
> *between you and the woman,*
> *and between your offspring and hers;*
> *he will crush your head,*
> *and you will strike his heel."*   Genesis 3:15

God declared here that one would come, born of a woman, who would ultimately destroy Satan's authority. This "one" was, of course, Jesus.

On that day, war was declared between Satan and women. This is something that the enemy understood and dreaded, but how many of us have really understood this. At that point, he unleashed a strategy to keep women bound through social, political, and even religious structures, keeping them enslaved under the power of his lies. This was to prevent them from understanding their true destiny and inheritance as ones who, through the power of Jesus, would crush Satan beneath their feet:

> *The God of peace will soon crush Satan under your*
> *feet.*   Romans 16:20

137

When I first came to God, I would read some of the controversial words Paul wrote about women in the church and be very confused. Anger, rejection, confusion, and indignation would wash over me like a wave. These verses did not make sense to me and certainly did not equate with the God I was beginning to know. Since then, I have been on a journey with these passages, seeking God for revelation, reading commentaries, and seeing the words in the context of the whole of God's Word, as well as the specific situation they were written for. I have come to the conclusion that my God loves women, He created us, and He wants to use us.

If you struggle with understanding these passages, seek God and His Word with a hunger for truth and with a heart of humility. Not understanding why the God who declares that He came to give us freedom would then supposedly hinder us from teaching or preaching about Him has caused much confusion and hurt in the heart of many of God's daughters. When God's own Word has been used by the enemy to oppress women, it can be quite confusing to know how we are to take hold of it with confidence. It can feel as if the sword is being pointed toward us, the sharp tip of the blade first. How, then, do we take it up?

We need to reclaim the words and promises of God over our lives, turning this pointed sword around, taking hold of it by the handle, and then turning it back onto our enemy. We can then face him and say, "I will not keep silent; I will not be held back any longer." It is time for the daughters of God to take hold of the sword which belongs to them and push back the lies and deception that have kept them bound.

As we mentioned early on, Psalm 68 refers to an army of women who proclaim the Word of the Lord, millions of Daddy God's daughters who will stand up and declare the truth about their Father over their own lives and the lives of others. This proclamation will cause the enemy to flee in haste, for it is what he has always dreaded. Warrior women, it is time for us to snatch back the sword out of the mouth of the enemy and use it to crush him under our feet. We can attest to what God has done for us boldly and without shame to those around us. Each of us has a story to tell, and we can speak in confidence that we overcome the accuser with the word of our testimony:

They overcame him
  by the blood of the Lamb
  and by the word of their testimony;
they did not love their lives so much
  as to shrink from death.   Revelation 12:11

The women of God cannot and shall not stay silent anymore, for the Father wants to release us in humility and in power. The sword belongs to us!

If we should ever doubt or question that God would use women to carry the sword, the Word of God, we need look no further than Mary, the very mother of Jesus. We know that Jesus is the embodiment of the Word of God, and when God was looking for someone to carry His Son, He chose this young woman. Mary literally carried the Word of God inside of her for nine months. What a breathtaking trust she was given!

All who follow Jesus are told that God deposits a measure of His Spirit inside of them (see Ephesians 1:13-14). We become carriers of the presence of God:

> *Don't you know that you yourselves are God's temple and that God's Spirit lives in you?*
>
> 1 Corinthians 3:16

Mary carried God's Word and presence inside of her, and we, men and women alike, have been given that same trust.

We know that the Word is a weapon, and a very powerful and effective one at that, but we must realize that this sword can also cause great damage if it is not used correctly or if it gets into the hands of the wrong persons. We can be like untrained and immature warriors, swinging our swords wildly, speaking out of season, or without the love of God. This can deeply wound others, leading them, not to repentance and closeness to God, but, instead, actually inoculating them against God's love.

God's truths are not always comfortable or easy, but we need to embrace both the kindness and severity of God in order to truly know Him. This is especially true when we are dealing with the truth about ourselves. We need to face the facts about our fallen nature, our inability to serve or even love God in our own strength. Let's ask Him to show us the depth of our need for Him. It is not always a pretty picture, and we have a tendency to run from the raw truth about ourselves.

God wants to shine His truth, to liberate us, not to condemn us. When we truly know the truth, we will then be so desperately aware of our need for God and His Holy Spirit as to enable us to become like Him. Then we will cling to the sword even more tightly and not even attempt to try to use our own carnal weapons.

Mary was chosen to carry the Word inside of her, but she was also told that a sword would pierce her own soul (see Luke 2:35). We can carry the Word as a weapon, but it is also necessary for us to allow it to pierce us and judge our hearts, revealing what is in them. In the Scriptures, the Word is described as a double-edged sword:

For the word of God is living and active. Sharper than any double-edged sword, it penetrates even to dividing soul and spirit, joints and marrow; it judges the thoughts and attitudes of the heart. Hebrews 4:12

If this sword is to work effectively, we must first freely surrender ourselves to the Lord Jesus, allowing Him to pierce our hearts with His sword, in order for Him to expose the division between soul and spirit, joints and marrow in our own lives. As we allow Him to do this in us, we can then take up this sword as an instrument to bring healing and freedom to others. Once Jesus has pierced us, we can be free from using the sword to wound and condemn others; instead, He can use us to preach the Good News of the kingdom.

141

Using and speaking God's Word is a great responsibility, which is why James says that those who teach will be judged more severely than others (see James 3:1). Let us know the Word Himself (Jesus), and then we will have the authority and humility to use the Word correctly and wisely. As warriors, let us be trained to use this sword mercilessly against the enemy of our souls, and yet let our words be seasoned with salt and grace to those around us—both within and without the church. Let us be *"wise as serpents and harmless* [innocent and gentle] *as doves"* (Matthew 10:16, NKJV).

God's Word is a love letter, a handbook for warriors, a Father's declaration of love, a history book, a law book, and our manual for living. As warrior women, this sword belongs to us, so let us take it up today and become skilled in the art of slaying dragons.

Warrior Women, Arise!

Chapter 12

FACING YOUR GIANTS

HAVE YOU EVER STRUGGLED WITH THE FEAR OF MAN or ever lived your life worrying about what others thought about you, bound by fear of their judgment and assessments? Have you conformed your personality to suit the demands of those around you? I know someone who can answer with a big YES to all of these questions, and that person is me. Talk about giants ... the fear of man has been mine.

Even as a young child, I was desperately afraid of other people and their opinions. I was afraid to go to school, to shops, to other people's houses for parties. I was even afraid to talk on the telephone. You name it, if it involved other people, I was terrified of it. Whenever I was out in public, I would sweat, my heart would beat fast, and my stomach would be tied in knots.

This fear followed me as I grew up, but I became more adept at hiding and handling it. I attempted to function in the adult world, dressing so as not to draw attention to myself, and controlling my behavior so as not to cause any offense or upset to anyone around me. Still, the fear would be so overwhelming at times that I was forced to resort to another tactic, that of hiding altogether. I would withdraw from activities, avoid making phone calls, and retreat further and further into my fortress of fear. I don't think I really understood at the time why I was so afraid, but I know now that this was all rooted in pride, a deep-seated fear of rejection, and an unquenchable need to be loved. Any of you who have experienced this terrible fear will know the snare that it can be:

> *Fear of man will prove to be a snare,*
> *but whoever trusts in the LORD is kept safe.*
>
> Proverbs 29:25

This Goliath has long been my worst and most powerful enemy, but the Lord has been gradually setting me free from it and revealing the courageous lioness He has placed inside of me. The Word assures us that *"perfect love drives out fear"* (1 John 4:18), and as I have allowed God to love me more, this fear has been driven from me.

This may sound like a beautiful and easy process, but in reality, it has been a battle and an extremely violent one at that. There were times when I felt like a wounded soldier lying bleeding on the battlefield and just wanting it all to end. Many times I was tempted to give up and doubted that God could ever remove this giant from my life. Yet, as a child of God, I know His promises. He has said:

> *For God has not given us a spirit of fear, but of power and*
> *of love and of a sound mind.*   2 Timothy 1:7, NKJV

No matter how great the pain or how brutal the battle, our Father has placed His power within us, to help us overcome. There is no weakness, wound, or sin with which we may struggle that the Holy Spirit cannot help us conquer. The Lord will strengthen, heal, forgive, and deliver us, but our responsibility is to surrender all to His will.

Recently, I watched the film *Nim's Island,* and I was touched by some of its scenes. In the movie, Jodie Foster plays the role of Alexandra Rover, a successful author who, despite writing fantastic adventure stories, suffers from agoraphobia and is so afraid of the outside world that she has not been out of her house for months and rarely opens the front door. On the other side of the world, there is a young girl named Nim who lives on an island with her father. Nim has a totally different outlook on life and has been trained by her father to understand that courage "is something we have to learn and relearn our whole lives. It is not just in you; it's in every choice we make each and every day." During the course of the film, these two connect with each other, first through correspondence, and later, in person.

Alexandra is bound up by fear, afraid to touch the world outside, and yet she finds an outlet for her true adventurous spirit through her books. The hero of her novels is a fictitious man named Alex Rover, and he is constantly involved in adventure and knows no fear. In this way, the writer lives out her desires for life vicariously through a fictional character she herself has created.

It came to me that this woman is just like many of God's daughters. We have dreams and longings for great adventure and destiny within us, and yet many times the only outlet we have for it all is in a kind of fantasy world. In reality, we often remain bound by fear and intimidation, never daring to live out our dreams and aspirations.

In the film, Alexandra is forced to leave her house and begin to overcome her worst fears because of the relationship she has developed with Nim. She feels that she must travel to Nim because the girl is wounded and alone (her father has been caught in a storm at sea). In this way, the author's desire to help someone in need outweighs and eventually conquers the terror that has imprisoned her. She is forced to fulfill the words she has written in her fictional books: "Be the hero of your own life story."

There are lessons for us all in this movie. When our focus is turned toward those around us who have a greater need than our own, we will be released and delivered from our own fears and Goliaths. Rover travels to save this young girl, but is, in turn, rescued in her own heart through opening up to another person. It took a young girl to unleash the hidden conqueror inside of the woman.

All of us have Goliaths in our lives. Yours may not be fear of man, as mine has been. Instead, it may be shame, pride, abuse, intimidation, worthlessness, unbelief, control, or something else. The list is endless. These Goliaths come against us, arousing fear and trembling in our hearts. They loom over us and taunt us with their apparent power and superiority. Often we dare not look them in the face, and in their presence we become over-whelmed with apprehension and dread.

It seems that we are trapped. We know that we cannot move forward unless these giants are overcome, but we are paralyzed by them and have no idea how we can face them successfully.

The well-known worship leader Rick Pino has writ-ten a powerful song about giants in his album, *Songs for an End-Time Army*. It is entitled "You're an Army." The chorus of it goes like this:

We cut off the giant's head;
We eat giants for our bread.

It continues:

You're an army dressed for battle;
Take the land, take the land.

These are extremely violent images, but somehow the warrior inside of me is stirred up when I hear these words. I don't want to be cowering somewhere, hiding from the giants in my life. I want to cut off their heads and eat them for my bread.

Destroying the works of the enemy in our own lives and in the lives of the people around us can and should be a daily occurrence. This is our end-time destiny as warriors. So, women of God, it is time to overcome the Goliaths in our lives. Too long they have been taunting us and holding us back from destiny. Goliath may shout, and he may roar, but his boisterous threats become as dust in the face of the living God.

Goliath, the Philistine champion whom David defeated (see 1 Samuel 17), was a giant and, therefore, intimidating, and yet his very largeness made him an easy target. Whatever it is that is standing in front of you, dare to look it right in the eye. The time for you to run or to be paralyzed with fear is over. Stand in the face of your enemy, and watch the deliverance your Lord will give you. Stand and watch as that which appeared impossible to overcome is obliterated in mere seconds.

Fear is actually only a spirit, an illusion, and yet it holds us in bondage and keeps us from action. Don't say that you cannot be like David or that you don't have his faith. David was just a simple shepherd boy who trusted his God. The Lord could have used any person present that day. He's not looking for men and women who are superheroes; He's looking for sons and daughters who are willing and obedient.

David was not even in the army at the time, so it wasn't his job to fight, and yet he was the only person there who dared to trust and proclaim the greatness of God. It was not about David, and it's not about us either. It is about allowing the power of God to flow through a human vessel. Jesus said that if we have faith as small *"as a mustard seed"* (one of the smallest seeds), we can move mountains (Matthew 17:20).

If you have chosen to give your life to Jesus, you are a daughter of the living God, and this means that you are made in His image. Therefore, the same Spirit who raised Jesus from the dead now lives within you (see Romans 8:11). The only thing that is holding you back is your beliefs about yourself. Of course you can defeat the enemies of God! The power of your Daddy, who made the heavens and the earth with just a few words from His mouth, lives inside of you. Don't let the judgments of others (or even your own) hinder you. You are not who they say you are. You are not weak, a failure, a mess, nor powerless. No, you are who God says you are; you are His child:

For you did not receive a spirit that makes you a slave again to fear, but you received the Spirit of sonship. And by him we cry, "Abba Father." Romans 8:15

It is He who has created you, and, therefore, it is only He who has authority to define you.

Shake off the shackles of shame and unworthiness. This is your hour to arise as a beautiful, powerful princess, God's warrior bride. Take up, out of the river of the Spirit of God, your stone of simple trust and intimacy with the Maker of the universe. Let the faithfulness and greatness of God replace your weakness and inferiority. Look your enemy in the face and proclaim, as David did:

"You come against me with sword and spear and javelin, but I come against you in the name of the LORD Almighty, the God of the armies of Israel, whom you

have defied. This day the LORD *will hand you over to me, and I'll strike you down and cut off your head."*

1 Samuel 17:45-46

Then leave your fear, hopelessness, and unbelief at the cross, throw your simple stone of faith, and watch as your Goliath sinks to the ground in utter defeat.

Warrior Women, Arise!

Chapter 13

THE RELUCTANT WARRIOR

PERHAPS SOME OF YOU FEEL FRIGHTENED OR hesitant when you hear all this talk about war and fighting. You may look at the state of your life today and feel so powerless and defeated that you cannot possibly understand how you would ever fight, let alone be victorious. Be encouraged, because that is exactly where God wants us when He calls us to enlist in His army. Then we are fully aware that we are not able to do this in our own strength and, therefore, will have to be reliant solely upon the grace and power of the cross to equip us.

God seems to like calling forth warriors in this helpless state. A great example is the case of Gideon. An angel of the Lord appeared to him and announced:

"The LORD is with you, mighty warrior." Judges 6:12

Up to that moment, Gideon had not been involved in any great battles (as far as we know), and he appeared shocked and troubled by this greeting. If he had been living in our times, he might have looked for the hidden camera, as this could only be a joke.

Gideon argued with the Lord, asking:

"How can I save Israel? My clan is the weakest in Manasseh, and I am the least in my family."

Judges 6:15

The Lord was not ready to engage in a discussion of Gideon's inabilities or fears. Instead, He assured His man:

"I will be with you, and you will strike down all the Midianites together." Judges 6:16

It seems obvious that the Lord was looking at the situation from a very different perspective than was Gideon. God was not looking at outward appearances or circumstances, but He was encouraging Gideon to understand that he had the potential (with His help) to change the destiny of his people.

Gideon was, no doubt, suffering from an inferiority complex. He was, after all, the youngest in his family and was from what was considered at the time to be the weakest clan in his entire tribe. He didn't seem to be the most suitable material for a mighty warrior, but the Spirit of God saw something else in him. He saw in Gideon what he was destined and called to be, what no one else, not even Gideon himself, could see, that in this man were the makings of a mighty warrior.

The Hebrew meaning of *Gideon* is "to fell a tree, destroy anything, cut down, warrior." So Gideon's name meant the very thing he was called to become.

It is very likely that Gideon was aware of the meaning

152

of his name, and this may have confused and aggravated him as he grew up. Perhaps he had been teased by other children who taunted him over his name. At the time the angel of the Lord found him, he was acting as anything but a brave warrior. If he had really had any of the traits of a warrior functioning in him at the time, I doubt very much that he would have been in hiding trying to press out a few grains of wheat for his family without the enemy seeing him and taking them.

You may identify with this. You may have had prophetic words spoken over your life, or even been given a name by parents or by God Himself that means something so opposite of who you are at the moment that it seems ridiculous. Perhaps these things have been little more than constant reminders of your inabilities and failures. Rather than listen to the voices of failure and defeat, it is time for us to allow the Spirit of God to speak His truth over our lives.

The enemies Gideon was called to defeat were the Midianites. This name, in the original Hebrew, meant "brawling, contention, discord, strife, a contest, or quarrel." The enemy is contesting our destiny too and has the desire of keeping us bound up in hopelessness and doubt.

The historical situation in which Gideon found himself was serious. For several hundred years the Israelites had been in a destructive cycle of forgetting their Lord, being handed over to their enemies, and then calling out to God for deliverance. In His compassion, the Lord would then raise up a hero to defeat their enemies, but, after the passage of time, the Israelites would rebel again, and the whole scenario was repeated.

Gideon had probably heard stories about the great heroes of the past and may have secretly aspired to be like them one day. And now, here was God Himself appointing him to be the next great hero to save the people of Israel from their enemies. But Gideon did not feel ready for this challenge, nor could he accept the fact that he was the man for the hour. He asked for heavenly confirmation on two different occasions, revealing his lack of faith in himself and in his ability to complete the task he was being called to do.

You may be a Gideon, someone who needs proof from God that He can use you at all, let alone that you can become a mighty warrior. Well, ask Him to confirm it, and He will. Dare to prove God, and you will not be disappointed.

Your doubts and questions need not hinder your destiny. It is better to be honest with God and get the matter established than to run away from your calling because you're afraid to question. You can be sure that whatever God has planned for you to accomplish for Him, you can do it. He does not make mistakes in whom He uses, for He loves to use *"the weak things of the world to shame the strong"* (1 Corinthians 1:27). In fact, God seems to be an expert at raising up the most unlikely people for every task. This is His speciality, for He looks at the heart and searches for one who will obey in childlike trust and give all the glory to Him for whatever is accomplished.

We know that faith pleases the Father, and yet He never condemns or turns away the one who is struggling with doubt. It is His kindness that will transform you and cause you to believe for the impossible. Trust Him today, but don't fear to approach Him with your doubts.

Maria Woodworth-Etter was a champion of the faith who was used mightily over a period of fifty years to fearlessly preach the Gospel. Wherever she traveled, healings, radical conversions, and even dramatic manifestations of the Holy Spirit followed. It was common, at her meetings, for participants of all ages and genders to receive divine visions, go into trances, and be overcome with a deep awareness of their sin. She was truly a prime example of a warrior woman. However, when she was called, she was just as reluctant and unbelieving as Gideon, if not more so.

Maria had sensed the Lord calling her to preach shortly after she was saved, but she saw no possibility of doing it, and so she just waited, biding her time. After all, she was a woman, she knew very little of the Bible, and she was living at the end of the 19th century, a time when women preachers were not only almost unheard of, but also not welcomed. She had everything going against her, but still the Lord called her.

Maria found herself being pulled between wanting to obey God and having to look at her weaknesses and her circumstances. She described her battle in her book *Signs and Wonders:* "There was all this time a secret monitor within telling me that I should be calling sinners to repentance. I could not get clear of that reflection by day or by night. Walking or dreaming, I seemed to have a large congregation before me, all in tears, as I told them the story of the cross. Thus for months and years did I debate; and yet did I falter and hesitate, and, like Jonah, trim my sail for Tarshish. I thought if I were a man it would be a pleasure for me; but for me, a woman, to preach, if I could, would subject me to ridicule and contempt among my friends and kindred and bring reproach upon His glorious cause." [1]

Despite the fact that Maria Woodworth-Etter had some understanding of who she was called to be, a mighty evangelist, she fought God in His choice of her. She had fears and doubts of her own, and she was also accused by the enemy, who tried to keep her from fulfilling her destiny. She wrote of this spiritual battle: "I longed to win a star for the Savior's crown. But when I thought of my weakness, I shrank from the work. Sometimes when the Spirit of God was striving and calling so plainly, I would yield and say, 'Yes, Lord: I will go.' The glory of God came upon me like a cloud, and I seemed to be carried away hundreds of miles and set down in a field of wheat, where the sheaves were falling all around me. I was filled with zeal and power and felt as if I could stand before the whole world and plead with dying sinners. It seemed to me that I must leave all and go at once.

"Then Satan would come in like a flood and say, 'You would look nice preaching, being a gazing stock for the people to make sport of. You know you could not do it.' Then I would think of my weakness and say, 'No, of course I cannot do it.' Then I would be in darkness and despair." [2]

If you know the Lord is calling you to fight in a certain area for Him, and you are resisting Him, precious woman, it is time to settle the issue. The world needs you, we need you, and your Father wants you. You can do it, with His help. Hold His hand today, resist the enemy's lies, and take your first step toward your ultimate purpose.

Maria Woodworth-Etter was later to shake whole areas of America with her dramatic anointing to call sinners to repentance. Countless souls were won as a result of her service, sick healed, and believers equipped and commissioned into worldwide ministry. She looked at herself and saw a weak, ungifted woman, while God saw His prime candidate to declare war on the powers of darkness that were holding people in bondage at that time. In the same way, Gideon was used to defeat the Midianite army in one night without ever using his sword.

You may also see only your lack of qualifications, but the world needs you to embrace your destiny, in whatever form it may take. Let the words of Maria Woodworth-Etter encourage and challenge you: "I knew that I was but a worm. God would have to take a worm to thresh a mountain. Then I asked God to give me the power He gave the Galilean fishermen—to anoint me for service. I came like a child asking for bread. I looked for it. God did not disappoint me." [3]

She continued, "Let me say, for the encouragement of those who are starting in the work of the Lord, God has promised to be with us always, even to the end. We are nothing but the clay that God speaks through. It is 'Not by might, but by my Spirit, saith the Lord of Hosts.'" [4]

Daughter of God, the enemy may shout, and you may doubt, but God can do what needs to be done. Take a first step and embrace His work for you today.

Warrior Women, Arise!

Chapter 14

THE WEEPING WARRIOR

*The world may despise brokenness, but remember—we are
not of this world. God will take the weak ones. If weeping
is a sign of weakness, God help us to weep!*

— Hattie Hammond [1]

I HAVE DONE A LOT OF WEEPING THROUGH THE
years, and so tears are a subject I am more than familiar
with. Most of mine have been tears of grief and sorrow
over my own life and the situations I found myself in, but
there have also been times when I wept for things that I
felt the Holy Spirit grieving over. I'll share a little secret
with you: In writing this book, there were times when it
felt as if I had done more weeping than writing! I wept
over my feelings of inadequacy for the task, over the pain
of the battle, and even for you who are reading these
pages, that the heart of our Father God would touch and
encourage you.

To weep is one of the most vulnerable acts a human being can engage in, and, as women, it is easy to feel that our
tears are futile and even worthy of scorn. Tears have many
times been associated with weakness, causing many, especially men, to feel ashamed or hindered in being able

to release them. I believe the Father wants to transform our concept of weeping and to disclose the value that our tears have with Him. We need not be ashamed of them. Rather, we can pour them out over the Lord, just as Mary poured out her perfume upon His feet.

Our tears are precious to the Lord, and, as David stated, God has kept each one of them in a bottle:

You have taken account of my wanderings;
Put my tears in Your bottle.
Are they not in Your book?   Psalm 56:8, NASB

Each one of our tears has been kept by the Lord and even recorded in His book. This should tell us something about their value to Him.

This practice of collecting tears in a bottle was a tradition of mourners in ancient Egyptian and Palestinian times. They then buried the bottle containing their tears of grief alongside the deceased, as a token of their love. The practice was still popular during Roman times, around the period Jesus walked the earth.

In Victorian times, the practice surfaced again, and mourners would store their tears in beautifully decorated vials. When the tears had evaporated, then the grieving process was thought to have been completed.

God stores our tears as an outward symbol of their value to Him, and through that act, He affirms that the substance they represent is worthy of capturing. This counters the notion that weeping is just a waste of time and energy.

The American poet John Vance Cheney wrote in his poem about tears: "The soul would have no rainbow had the eyes no tears." [2] I love this image, as it symbolizes the hope that can come after a time of weeping and how the faithfulness and beauty of God can arise out of great suffering.

King David put it like this:

Weeping may remain for a night,
but rejoicing comes in the morning.   Psalm 30:5

Tears represent the outward manifestation of mankind's sorrow and their ability to express grief and vulnerability. A God who is acquainted with suffering Himself could never despise this expression.

There are, of course, many forms of tears, those cried in self-pity, anger, despair, shock, and sorrow, and, paradoxically, even during times of joy. Tears are a gift to us in this fallen world as a means to deal with the suffering and pain that exists. Tears that are induced through emotions contain hormones, one of which is a natural painkiller, so they even bring about a physical release and comfort to us.

Tears have a cleansing function, not only removing impurities by their actual presence, but also serving to purify our souls.

The tender heart of God is moved through our tears. Take the case of Hagar, Sarah's Egyptian maidservant. Sarah had forced her husband, Abraham, into having a child with Hagar. Later on, however, Sarah became jealous of Hagar and wanted to have her and her son, Ishmael, sent away. Abraham did send them away, and Hagar and her son found themselves lost in the desert. In great pain and desperation, both Hagar and Ishmael wept bitterly. The reaction of God to their tears was not condemnation or silence:

> *God heard the boy crying, and the angel of God called to Hagar from heaven and said to her, "What is the matter, Hagar? Do not be afraid; God has heard the boy crying as he lies there. Lift the boy up and take him by the hand, for I will make him into a great nation."*
>
> Genesis 21:17-18

This story reveals the compassion and mercy of God in response to the suffering of His creation. Even when our tears are a result of our own disobedience and sin or that of those around us, our God is not deaf to our weeping.

If the enemy has accused you over your tears, don't listen any longer to his taunts. Just as we are created to birth new life, so we are called to weep. Submit your emotions to Jesus, and do not despise your vulnerability. It is your very desperation and need which touches the heart of God and causes Him to arise on your behalf.

Smith Wigglesworth was a British healing evangelist who was used mightily by God across the earth in supernatural healings and miracles. After a series of very successful meetings in New Zealand, he was asked by a pastor what the secret to his great power was. Wigglesworth replied: "I am sorry you asked me that question, but I will answer it. I am a brokenhearted man. My wife, who meant everything to me, died eleven years ago. After the funeral, I went back and lay on her grave. I wanted to die there. But God spoke to me and told me to rise up and come away. I told him if He would give me a double portion of the Spirit—my wife's and my own—I would go and preach the Gospel. God was gracious to me and answered my request. But I sail the high seas alone. I am a lonely man, and many a time all I can do is weep and weep." [3]

This man moved in such supernatural power that he shook every nation he visited, yet here he proclaims that God's strength was made perfect in his weakness. It was his very brokenness and dependence upon God which was the key to his success. His tears were not shed in vain.

I believe God is wanting to take us to the place where we receive healing from our wounds and mistakes and where our weeping for the past ceases and is replaced with a harvest of joy. As He turns our mourning into dancing, we can then turn ourselves toward heaven and seek to know the heart of God and enter into the honor of weeping for that which resides in His heart.

Jesus lived as a holy man on this earth, and yet He knew what it was to weep. He was not ashamed to release His grief when Lazarus died, and, as He stood outside the tomb of His friend, the Bible states frankly:

Jesus wept.   John 11:35

In some ways, this act of Jesus could be seen as futile, especially when we know that He was about to raise Lazarus from the dead. Yet I believe there is a hidden key for us here, as women warriors, about how to overcome the powers of darkness and circumstances that may appear hopeless. Jesus wept because He shared in the grief of those around Him, and He poured out His tears in compassionate intercession to the Father.

After weeping, Jesus then prayed:

> *"Father, I thank you that you have heard me. I knew that you always hear me, but I said this for the benefit of the people standing here, that they may believe that you sent me."* John 11:41-42

After speaking these words, Jesus turned to Lazarus's tomb and commanded him to come out, and Lazarus emerged, with his body still wrapped in strips of linen. I would suggest that God heard the tears Jesus wept and was moved to act, causing a miraculous change in the situation. Jesus' tears were not wasteful but, rather, acted as intercession, which reversed the curse of death.

Queen Esther also found herself in a situation which appeared hopeless, as a decree had been issued through which her people, the Jews, were to be eradicated. She wept before the king in order to gain his help for them:

> *Esther again pleaded with the king, falling at his feet and weeping. She begged him to put an end to the evil plan of Haman the Agagite, which he had devised against the Jews.* Esther 8:3

The result of Esther's weeping was this:

Then the king extended the gold scepter to Esther and she arose and stood before him.　　　　Esther 8:4

As women warriors, our tears, sent up to the throne room of God, can change circumstances and cause the heart of the Father to be moved. We can weep tears for others, sharing in the Lord's grief over the state of the world, and then allow those tears to be poured out toward His throne room as prayer.

The Israelites were even commanded to bring forth the weeping women and to teach their daughters to weep, in order to bring about repentance throughout the nation in sin and rebellion against God:

This is what the LORD Almighty says:
　"Consider now! Call for the wailing women to come;
　　send for the most skillful of them.
Let them come quickly
　and wail over us
till our eyes overflow with tears
　and water streams from our eyelids."
　　　　　　　　　　　　　Jeremiah 9:17-18

One of our end-time missions may be to weep before the Lord for His grace and mercy over a fallen world and to intercede on behalf of those who are living in defiance and pride toward the living God. Tears will be a formidable weapon for the warrior, and, in this way, apparent weakness will be turned into great victory.

We can carry tears as seeds, confident that as we sow with them, we will reap in joy:

> *Those who sow in tears*
>   *will reap with songs of joy.*
> *He who goes out weeping,*
>   *carrying seed to sow,*
> *will return with songs of joy,*
>   *carrying sheaves with him.*   Psalm 126:5-6

We can weep tears for others, sharing in the grief of God over the state of the world and allowing them to be poured out to the throne room as prayer.

We need to teach our daughters to weep, to travail for the things of God, and, as weeping warriors, to truly be used as God's secret weapon in prayer.

Powerful woman evangelist and missionary Gwen Shaw, who started the organization known as End-Time Handmaidens and Servants, has been ministering for more than fifty years now. A number of years ago the Holy Spirit spoke to her that it was time to teach the people of God how to weep. In her *End-Time Handmaidens and Servants Magazine*, she wrote, "My Bible says to the women of our churches, '*Hear the word of the* LORD, *O ye women, and let your ear receive the word of his mouth, and teach your daughters wailing and every one her neighbor lamentation*' (Jeremiah 9:20, KJV).

"God is commanding you older women, who still know how to travail and weep for souls, not to lay down this life-saving call of God and these gifts which He has given you, but to teach our spiritual daughters and our neighbors (the other women of the Church) how to travail again, like we used to in the old days ... .

"We women were born to travail. This call is to us; let us rise to the occasion! 'Let our eyes run down with tears and our eyelids gush out with waters' (Jeremiah 9:18)." [4]

To *travail* means to be in intense prayer over an issue, as if in the pangs of childbirth. Paul wrote to the Galatian church about this form of prayer:

My dear children, for whom I am again in the pains of childbirth until Christ is formed in you ... .

Galatians 4:19

He also described this deep sort of prayer in his letter to the Roman believers:

In the same way, the Spirit helps us in our weakness. We do not know what we ought to pray for, but the Spirit himself intercedes for us with groans that words cannot express. Romans 8:26

We can allow the Holy Spirit to pray and weep through us, bringing about changes in individual lives, as well as among the nations. I believe that God wants to release us, as weeping warriors, leaving behind the shame of our past and using our tears as powerful weapons in His hand. Let the weeping warriors now arise in dignity and strength.

Warrior Women, Arise!

Chapter 15

THE SINGLE WARRIOR

I HAVE A NUMBER OF FRIENDS WHO ARE NOT married, and one of them in particular asked me to write a chapter for the single women in the church. She shared with me some of the difficulties single Christian women encounter, and I came to realize that it is easy to overlook singles when discussing certain topics, as the focus tends to be on those who are married and/or have children. This should not be, as single women account for about a quarter of evangelical churchgoers, including those who are divorced or widowed. So I will try to address all three of these categories in order. I understand that how life looks for you as a single, can be incredibly diverse, but my prayer is that you will be encouraged to see that you more than qualify to enter into the army of God, regardless of your particular marital status.

THE UNMARRIED SINGLE WARRIOR

Mennonite theologian John Howard Yoder has written, "It needs to be taught as normative Christian truth that singleness is the first normal state for every Christian." [1] He's right. A great number of Christian women are single, either by choice or circumstance. Still, the message that women need to be married in order to be fully used by God is often broadcast in the church. The result is that many Christian singles can be made to feel like second-class citizens.

In his book *The Single Issue,* Al Hsu wrote, "Many singles have the vague sense that singleness is a temporary phase, and that 'real life' begins at marriage. For this reason, they put life on hold, waiting until a mate comes along before really living life." [2] If you are single, perhaps you can relate to this.

Jesus shattered many notions about singleness in the culture of His day. He was single Himself; yet He served His God wholeheartedly. The fact that He lived as both God and man meant that He was able to understand and sympathize with us in our weaknesses. Jesus knew what it felt like to long for another with whom to share His life. He also knew that His life was not His own, and He was able to direct all His needs and longings toward His Father to be met. In this way, He lived a fulfilled and fruitful life as a single man and accomplished the will of God the Father through His obedience.

Marriage is not an eternal state. It is a gift given here on earth, but it is not required or given to all. Al Hsu further stated in his book, "Marriage is not the starting point for 'real life.' Salvation in Christ is. And all who have come to Christ have already begun to participate in the abundant life Jesus came to give us." [3]

Paul's teachings on marriage and singleness were also very radical. He did not elevate one state over the other, but rather laid a foundation for knowing that both are equally acceptable and valued routes for an individual to choose as a follower of Jesus. Jesus's example and, later, the teachings of Paul were revolutionary for youth who wanted an alternative to the married life, as something desirable and honorable.

It is natural for most of us to long for a partner. It can be very painful for those of you who are serving God faithfully but long to be married, and no one is showing up on the horizon for you. Perhaps you have prayed for years, wept many bitter tears, heard the promise quoted, *"Delight yourself in the LORD and he will give you the desires of your heart"* (Psalm 37:4), and, quite frankly, you are fed up. The years are ticking by, and the waiting is almost beyond your ability to bear. Bitterness and doubt may have crept in, which are affecting your relationship with and service for your Lord. I have no easy answers for you, but one thing I am sure of: You do not need a husband to become part of God's end-time army.

In fact, even though you might not like to hear it, you have an advantage over those of us who are married. Paul states that it is better not to be married. The one who is married, he says, is concerned with keeping their partner happy, and this can distract them from total devotion to the Lord (see 1 Corinthians 7:28-35). Single woman, you have a leg up. You can know God so radically and intimately that you don't even have time to think about a man.

There is a stereotype, enforced by many romantic comedies and literature, that we will find our prince and live happily ever after in a blissful state of ecstasy and belonging. This picture can often cloud our ideals, especially as a single, and cause us to be ever looking out for Mr. Perfect to appear and save the day. However, as any married woman will tell you, Mr. Perfect lives only on the screen and in pocketbook romance novels! Marriage will never complete us; only Jesus can do that. A husband may meet many of our emotional, sexual, and companionship needs, but he can never take the place of our Lord. I think that many times, both as singles and married women, we tend to forget this. We can place unrealistic expectations on our men, by thinking that they can meet all our hopes and needs. Men are just as incomplete as we are, and they were never meant to save the day for us.

All of this being said, the Lord loves you so tenderly and sees your longing to be loved by a man, so continue to pour out your frustration upon Him. However, if He is your Lord, He is the one who will decide if and when you marry. Perhaps you need to lay this whole area of your life on the altar again today and leave it in His hands. He will help you, for He understands your pain.

Some of you cannot relate to this longing at all. Perhaps you are angry and even annoyed with all this talk of marriage. You may not be interested in finding a husband, but, rather, want to be recognized and accepted for who you are as a person. This is a genuine and admirable desire, for you are complete without a husband. You are a child of God and have the Creator of the universe living inside of you.

Never before in the history of the world have women been at such an advantage, for this is one of the first times in history when it is more or less socially acceptable for a woman not to marry and yet be successful in the world. You are of equal value to married women, and you are much needed in the church and in the community. The Lord most certainly does not see you as a second-class citizen.

A modern-day example of a single warrior woman is a lady named Michele Perry. Michele is currently living in one of the most violent and poor places on the earth—the Sudan. She started a ministry there in 2006, after being ordained by Iris Ministries (run by Heidi and Ronald Baker). Michele is young, in her early thirties, single, and has only one leg, but none of these facts deters her (or God) from fulfilling her calling to the Sudan. She now looks after more than two hundred children in four centers and helps to give education to more than five hundred. Her ministry has started fourteen churches, and she is actively involved in rescuing children from sex trafficking. She faces danger to her body, soul, and spirit on a daily basis, yet she chooses to fight courageously for those around her who have no defense.

Michele wars with the radical, unconditional love and power of the Lord Jesus though simple daily steps of obedience. In an interview with Sid Roth on his television program *It's Supernatural,* Perry was asked how a person could take the step to move to the Sudan without any money, plans, or protection. She answered with the following words, "Look into the eyes of the One who is

Love, and you fall in love, and you let Him love you, past the place of your fear and past the place of your pain and love you until you become the face and expression of His love to those around you. Then you'll go anywhere because you're in love." [4]

You may not be called to the Sudan, but you have a unique purpose and gift to give to this world. You may not be married, but you are already spoken for by the King of all Kings, Jesus. He is your Bridegroom, and He loves you with such a passionate and unconditional love, far beyond that which any man could offer you. Whether you will eventually marry or not, you are complete in Christ today, and your place in the army of God is settled. All that remains is for you to seek the Father and find out which battleground He has for you to bring the victory of the cross to.

THE DIVORCED SINGLE WARRIOR

I know that many of you reading this book may be divorced, through either your own choice or your partner's. You, therefore, have experienced marriage, and now you are single again, and this can be a painful position to be in. Not only do you deal with the agony of lost love (perhaps through betrayal, abuse, or mistakes of your own), but there is also the issue of others' reactions. There can be an aura of shame surrounding divorced women in the church, and this can create in you a feeling that your chances of being used by God are over.

You may sit in the church pew and cower, hoping no one will confront you, or maybe you stay at home and don't even dare to show your face in church anymore, because of the stigma and sting of divorce. Perhaps you are so filled with a sense of failure that you are paralyzed in your walk with Jesus, and previous dreams lie shipwrecked on the island of loneliness you find yourself on. It could be that the process of divorce has left you embittered toward men and cynical toward the whole concept of love and intimacy.

Our God is a God of covenant, and divorce is something which cuts across His longing for commitment and love. However, He is also the God of redemption, and no matter the extent of the mistakes in your life or that of your partner in this situation, the cross of Jesus is wide enough to cover them. Whatever your state at this time, the Lord of Hosts is with you. He does not reject divorced women.

Just think about the woman at the well. Did you know that she was actually the first recorded evangelist in the Bible? After her short meeting with Jesus, she went back to her town and told the people there all about Him, and many began to believe on Him because of her testimony (see John 4). Most of us know the story. This was the woman to whom Jesus spoke about streams of living water and true worship. Well, let's look a little closer at her life.

The first strike against this woman was that she was a Samaritan, the second that she was a woman, and the third that she had been divorced five times and was now living with a sixth man. She was clearly not the most likely candidate for the first evangelist in the ministry of Jesus.

The fact that Jesus even talked to this woman was revolutionary in itself. At that time, Samaritans were considered, by the Jewish people, to be as low as dogs. Respectable Jews certainly never spoke to them.

Women were not much higher on the scale, and it was not common at all for a Jewish man to address a woman who was not his wife in this manner.

To add to all this, the woman in question had lived a shameful and sinful life. This might explain why she was at the well at this particular time of day. Coming at this odd hour enabled her to avoid the accusing and judging eyes of the other women in the community, who came early in the morning to get water for their daily chores.

Still, Jesus not only spoke to the woman, but had with her His longest recorded conversation. And, what's more, in the process of their conversation, He began to divulge to this woman precious secrets about worship.

At no point did the Lord seem to have any problem with talking to a divorced woman and then entrusting her with some privileged information and some privileged tasks. So, if you have harbored any doubts about your ability or qualification as an end-time warrior, this story should cause you to think again. Our God is the most revolutionary being in this universe. He scorns the politically-correct attitudes of the culture of the day and is passionately concerned with transforming broken, sinful lives into masterpieces of His grace and love.

Jesus believes in women. He believes in our capacity to understand spiritual matters, and appears not to have the slightest hesitation in raising us up in service to Him. I believe that He looked beyond the behavioral failures of the woman at the well and saw, instead, her capacity as a worshiper and warrior. I believe He saw in her a frustrated warrior, one whom He had endued with great talents and abilities. Perhaps it was in her frustration that the woman had turned to men as the only release for the greatness she carried inside of her. But a few minutes' meeting with Jesus, and her true capacity was unleashed.

If you are divorced, that is something that has happened to you, but it does not need to define you. If there are areas where you need to repent and receive healing, don't hesitate, because there is destiny locked up inside of you. Today, Jesus is meeting you at the well of your need, calling you forth, and commissioning you to go out and declare what He has done for you. Welcome, warrior woman. Take your place with dignity and honor in the army of God.

THE WIDOWED SINGLE WARRIOR

There may be some of you reading this book who are single because death has taken the one you love. For you, grief is very real and intense and, in your loss, perhaps you find yourself living in the past, where you were one with your husband. It may be unfathomable for you to imagine yourself accomplishing a work for

Jesus without your husband. Here again, Jesus is able to meet you in whichever phase of the grieving process you are in. You and your husband will be reunited one day, but, for now, Jesus has chosen to keep you on this earth.

Naomi and Ruth are encouraging examples in this regard. Naomi had lost her husband and both of her sons, and the grief she felt must have been overwhelming. Not surprisingly, she asked to be called *Mara*, which means "bitter," rather than her real name, *Naomi*, which means "pleasant." She had followed her husband to a foreign land and was now left bereft, without him or her sons.

Ruth, a young widow herself at this point, chose to follow her mother-in-law to the land of Naomi's birth. Together they undertook a long and dangerous journey, especially as single women traveling alone.

In those days, being a widow was a crippling and vulnerable position to be in, as it was the man's task to provide for the wife, and without him she could starve. These women, however, were not hindered by their circumstances, but repeatedly showed prudence, boldness, and faith, as they sought to fend for themselves. They were truly warriors who fought for survival, trusting in the intervention of a faithful God to provide for them. Little did either of them realize that they were actually being used to shape the destiny of a nation and even facilitate the eventual coming of the Savior into the world. The acts of courage and boldness on the part of Naomi and Ruth in approaching Boaz resulted in Ruth's marriage to him and, subsequently, the birth of a baby, Obed. This baby was to be the grandfather of King David, of the bloodline through which Jesus came.

On a personal level, the grief and shame of these two women was replaced with honor and comfort. On a deeper level, they made a way for a child to be born, who was of the lineage through which Jesus would come.

Jesus can also turn your mourning into joy and raise you up to change world history. He can transform your bitterness of soul into something pleasant, not only for you, but also for those around you. Does that sound too radical and unbelievable? I'm sure Naomi and Ruth were amazed at the far-reaching consequences of their simple acts of obedience and trust. I imagine the enemy was just as shocked, as he realized that two women, who represented the weakest and least influential elements of society at the time, were used to bring forth the very One who would bring about his ultimate defeat. It is in your hiddenness and apparent defeat that Jesus can turn the tables and crush the head of the enemy through you.

Lavinia Bartlett, a woman who lived during the Victorian era in England, is an illuminating example of a widow used by God in this way. At the time, Charles Spurgeon, the famous preacher, had one of the largest churches of the day at Metropolitan Tabernacle in London. Spurgeon said of Bartlett, "My best deacon is a woman," [5] powerful and honoring words from such a man of faith. Yet, how did this physically weak widow woman come to be known in this way?

Lavinia Bartlett showed signs of greatness early in life, starting a school for village girls at the tender age of fourteen. The school grew in popularity, and as Bartlett matured, she turned the school into a business, teaching the girls a form of embroidery, which led to employment for more than two hundred girls and women. She was known not only for her ingenuity, but also as "The Praying Woman." [6] Later, she married, had two boys, and settled down to a relatively quiet life, directing much of her energy toward prayer for her sons.

Then, in 1853, Lavinia Bartlett was left a widow. To further complicate her situation, she had developed a heart complaint, which left her incredibly frail at times, and, with two teenaged boys to care for, her future did not look bright. But it was at this point in time that her calling as a warrior for souls took shape as never before. She was asked to step in and take a Sunday school class for women at Spurgeon's church one Sunday. She started with a class of three teenagers, and after six years, the number had swelled to between seven and eight hundred women.

Mrs. Bartlett taught, inspired, and implored these women almost every Sunday for fifteen years to follow Jesus courageously, and brought many to salvation. Her life impacted thousands of people, and yet she lived each week in great weakness and dependence upon her God, due to her ill health.

Lavinia Bartlett may have been a sick widow, yet she did not allow her circumstances to deter her from the calling of God upon her life. She poured herself out as a living sacrifice. Charles Spurgeon said of her, "Love was the secret of her power. Tears flowed from many eyes when she pleaded, because her soul was stirred within her." [7]

Her testimony still speaks, revealing how God can take the broken and contrite places in our hearts and use them mightily for His glory. No matter how deep your pain and grief, there is nothing that can hold you back from being a warrior woman for Jesus—not even death itself.

Warrior Women, Arise!

Chapter 16

THE MARRIED WARRIOR

THE FILM ENTITLED *MR. AND MRS. SMITH*, STARRING Brad Pitt and Angelina Jolie, was a great hit. The story line is as follows: A man and his wife, who appear to live an ordinary and rather mundane life, have grown bored with each other. The truth is gradually revealed that they are actually both undercover hit agents. In other words, they are paid to kill, but they have hidden this secret life from each other, and it is this very deception that is destroying their relationship. Both seem to have been created for action and feel suffocated when they cannot share this side of themselves with their partner.

As the plot thickens, they discover that they have been assigned to kill each other, and after years of pent-up rage, they decide to do it. Eventually they realize that their true enemy lies outside of themselves, and they join forces to fight against that enemy. As they fight together, their love and passion for one another is reignited. I am not endorsing everything in this film or saying that we are called to be killers, but I believe there is some hidden truth here for us to glean.

With Christian couples, both the man and the woman are born to be warriors and are destined to fight for a cause outside of themselves and to destroy the works of the enemy on this earth. When we are not functioning in these gifts or we keep them hidden from each other, we can become bored. In these moments, the enemy will try to get us to direct our frustrations toward one another, rather than at him. This is exactly where many Christian marriages find themselves today: two frustrated and bored warriors, spending their time shooting at each other, rather than joining forces against Satan.

When the Mr. and Mrs. Smiths in the Christian world are unveiled as the Mr. and Mrs. Warriors, change will occur. We were destined to be caught up in the adventure of preaching the Gospel and shooting down the enemy's missiles, not waging war against our spouses.

What we do know is that God has promised to pour out His Spirit *"on all people"* (Joel 2:28), and just as He did with Adam and Eve, God wants to raise up men and women together to fight and subdue the earth. We have a great commission, and as a married couple we can strengthen, encourage, and complement each other to embrace our destiny. Sadly, this is not always the case, as competition, suppression, control, and manipulation often enter into the picture, causing problems.

I have spoken to a number of friends about this whole matter of being a wife and a warrior and, to be honest, it is not an easy topic in many ways. One of my friends said to me recently, "I really want to be a warrior for Jesus, but how does it work with the whole issue of submission?" It's a good question, and one that is not easily answered. Perhaps you have asked the same or similar questions yourself.

This can be complicated when, as wives, we believe that God is calling us to accomplish something for Him, something that our husbands may not understand or endorse. What do we do in these cases? We want to obey our God and, at the same time, not force our own will. It creates a sensitive situation, to say the least, but it is not an impossible one.

The whole concept of submission and even the word itself is, in many ways, like an explosive missile, often causing extreme reactions. *Submit* is a word that, apart from the Christian world, is almost unused today, and, therefore, it carries with it many prejudices and emotive responses. Much of the negative response to this word stems from a lack of understanding of its true meaning, and this is further complicated by the way the concept has been twisted and abused in order to suppress women. Speaking honestly, I think that many of us cringe when we hear the word *submit*.

I actually did not want to write this chapter at all and thought I would just skip over the whole issue of submission for a later date. (Don't ask me what that date might have been ... maybe when I got around to writing about Never-Never Land).

"Why am I resisting this?" I finally asked myself. It was because I was afraid. I wanted to encourage women, but I knew I didn't have all the answers myself. This is such a difficult area for all of us anyway because of the ancient wound between men and women, which we discussed in Chapter 6.

In order to stay on track in this subject, we must go back to the character of our Creator and remind ourselves of His ultimate goal in establishing marriage in the first place. As with everything God has prepared for us, marriage was intended to be a blessing, and it was to depict a beautiful picture of mutual trust, respect, and love between two of God's creatures. As we noted earlier, Eve was created for Adam as a *"suitable helper,"* because God saw that it was not good for man to be alone (see Genesis 2:18 and 20). She was to complement and strengthen him, as the perfect gift from a loving Creator. She stood as his equal in the eyes of God, representing part of His image.

At this point, there was no competition between Adam and Eve, but after the Fall, things changed, and the harmony and order that originally reigned in their relationship was broken (see Genesis 3). God has, therefore, set up guidelines to protect men and women in their fallen state and to restore divine order to their relationship.

At the Fall, Adam failed to stand with and protect Eve and, therefore, God now urges men to love and serve their wives, and not neglect them and fail to care for them properly. Eve made a major, destructive decision without consulting Adam; consequently, God now leads women to respect and submit to their husbands (especially when no agreement can be found in a decision-making process), thus preventing women from making further harmful decisions on their own. These guidelines are not meant to suppress or hinder us, but rather, to protect us from the consequences of sin and guard us from the enemy's schemes.

These issues are crucial in the area of warfare, as there needs to be order in our marriages, if we are to successfully stand against the enemy. Depending on how deep the wound from men, perhaps our own husbands, they can evoke some pretty intense emotions. Submission is a threat to our will, to the popular concept of "me, me, me"; it involves trust, and it has been badly abused. But if we are to arise as God's warrior women in this hour, we need to address this area. If we don't, there is a danger that we will end up in the same ditch as the feminists. They took freedom by force, but God wants us to embrace it as a gift, with humility and boldness. We must ultimately submit to Jesus in this and trust that He will take the land for us and make a way where there seems to be no way.

The concept of submission is always mentioned in the Scriptures in the context of the need for order and respect, and it is an act requested of us out of our free will and never out of control. For example, all of us, men and women alike, are told to submit to God (see James 4:7), young men are told to be submissive to older men (see 1 Peter 5:5), all should submit to the governing authorities (see Romans 13:1), believers should submit to their leaders (see Hebrews 13:17), as Christians we should submit to one another (see Ephesians 5:21), and, finally, wives should submit to their husbands as the church submits to Christ (Ephesians 5:22-24). In all of these cases, it is an act of free will, done in obedience to God, and it speaks of an attitude of humility, honor, and respect. We choose to lay down our own will in order to prefer another. This we do as liberated adults and not as a result of others demanding it of us. It is also clear that in all cases we can never submit to anyone or anything that involves sin or goes against our conscience.

What is strange is that we focus so much on these words to women and fail to focus more on the words spoken to men in the context of marriage, for there we see provision by a loving Father for creating an atmosphere of complete safety:

Husbands, love your wives, just as Christ loved the church and gave himself up for her to make her holy, cleansing her by the washing with water through the word.
In this same way, husbands ought to love their wives as their own bodies. He who loves his wife loves himself.

Ephesians 5:25-26 and 28

What greater thing could we experience than being loved by a man who looks after us just as Jesus cares for His church! And how does Jesus care for His church? He loves us as He does His own body, freely laying down His life to serve and care for us. It is unlikely that submission would be much of an issue if our husbands loved us in this way. Also, if both of us, husbands and wives alike, were to obey the command *"Submit one to another in love,"* we would be consistently laying down our lives for one another and always preferring the other in love.

Mary, the mother of Jesus, is a courageous and comforting example for us in the whole area of submission.

First, as a very young girl, she received a message of destiny from an angel, and, without hesitating, she laid down her will to favor the plan of God:

> *"I am the Lord's servant .... May it be to me as you have said."*   Luke 1:38

When Mary made this decision to submit to the Lord's will, she must have understood that it could very well cost her everything: her reputation, family, friends, future, and even her life. At that time, according to Jewish law, a woman could be stoned for becoming pregnant before marriage. Because of this, Mary would have been fully justified in pouring out complaints and arguments to the Lord, but, instead, she responded with simple trust and obedience. She was a true warrior of faith.

Mary embraced her God-given destiny, but then she had to share it with her husband-to-be, Joseph. God alone knows how hard it must have been for her to try to explain to this man that she was the first woman ever recorded to have become pregnant through divine conception, without the cooperation of a man. We do not know exactly what was said between them, but we understand, from Joseph's response, that he did not believe her. He was planning to divorce her privately,[1] so as not to bring disgrace upon her (indicating that he also still cared for her, but was not willing to be involved or bless the seed of destiny she claimed to be carrying in her womb). This must have been a terribly testing and worrying time for Mary. She was now totally reliant upon the same God who had spoken to her in the first place, to speak to Joseph.

This is where we can glean so much revelation and encouragement from Mary's story for our present lives. If God comes and begins to reveal His end-time purpose for us, depositing the seed of destiny within our spirits, we need not fear our husbands' response. We can cry out, in trust that the same revelation sent to Joseph will come to our husbands. Joseph was given one of many dreams, in which God confirmed and affirmed that which Mary had told him. We can trust that no matter how radical a message our Lord speaks, He will be faithful to back us up.

Joseph was a man who obeyed the word of the Lord immediately. And we can be sure that if God is calling us to rise up as warriors, the Holy Spirit is wanting to do the same with our husbands.

Another example for us is Deborah. The little we know about her private life, including the name of her husband, begins in Judges 4:4:

Deborah, a prophetess, the wife of Lappidoth, was leading Israel at that time.

So Deborah was a married woman, despite the fact that she was a prophetess, a political leader, and even a warrior. This must have been a challenging and unusual marriage for those days, as Deborah was the one who was in the forefront. She must have had an encouraging and humble husband, one who was willing to bless and support his wife in her God-given call. The only clue as to his nature is given in his name, *Lappidoth*. The Hebrew meaning of this name is "to shine, burning lamp, flame, torch." For me, this is a beautiful and honoring picture of what God has for husbands of warrior women. The position of influence and authority his wife enjoyed did not cause him to live in her shadow, but, rather, he was a man who shone in his own right. This speaks prophetically to me that as we are released as warriors and supported by our husbands, rather than causing them to be hindered, they will actually shine in the destiny that God has for them. This may not happen overnight, and in cases where there is wounding or rebellion in the heart of our husbands and/or in us, there may be a struggle.

I am so thankful that God has given me a husband with the heart of Lappidoth. Olof is truly a man who shines for Jesus, yet he has never used his gifts or torch to try to shut me down. He has always been my biggest fan. He has believed in me, even when I had no faith in myself, and gently, yet persuasively, encouraged me to dare to enter into new arenas. He has truly been an example of a husband who serves and loves his bride as Jesus loves the church, and, through his unconditional love, has taught me so much about the heart of Jesus for me.

Before you get the idea that we have the perfect marriage, know that we are not without our conflicts. Our personalities and giftings are radically different from each other. I am, in many ways, like a speedboat, easily moved and ready for action, while he is more like a steamboat. He travels at a steady, balanced pace and does not change course easily or quickly. Herein lies the source for potential conflicts and opportunities for me to practice the art of submission.

Not long after we were married, the first case of differing wills surfaced. We had been sent a leaflet about a prayer conference in the mail, and as soon as I opened it, I knew that we were to supposed to attend. I did not have any logical arguments to back up my knowing. I just knew deep down in my spirit that it was right. I was used to following God in this fashion, trusting my intuition and spirit. I was, therefore, shocked when my husband did not share my enthusiasm or conviction at all. He was accustomed to logically and prayerfully making decisions and requiring a period of time, even days, before he came to any conclusion. In this case, he was also concerned that we didn't have the money for the trip.

I remember how frustrated and outraged I was at this. I could not believe that he was refusing to understand that God had spoken to me. I was also afraid that we would end up disobeying God in the matter, as I was so sure it was His will for us to attend the conference.

I wanted to push my case and come to a decision right then and there, but I sensed God saying to me, "Just wait, Amanda." I felt, therefore, that I was to be quiet and submit, trusting that God would speak to my husband Himself. I still remember the agony of those few days. It felt nearly impossible for me to keep my mouth shut, and I so wanted to help God out in persuading my husband as to His will.

Somehow, by the grace of God, I was able to endure, and eventually Olof informed me that he felt peace about us going to the conference. I was relieved, but also shaken, as I realized that life was not going to be the same for me now that I was married. I could no longer make major decisions without my husband, and each of us seemed to approach the whole process very differently.

We have been married for more than fourteen years now, and we are still learning to make room for our differences and to flow with one another. Most of the time, we practice the art of submitting to each other. There have actually been very few cases in which we have had radically opposing viewpoints and where I have had to submit. In almost every one of these cases, I needed to receive more revelation about the situation and/or allow time for Olof to embrace the concept in his own manner.

I can't say that I find this process easy or pleasant, especially at the time, but it usually works more character and patience in me, qualities I can always improve in. The message is that marriage works best when we are both submitted to the Holy Spirit, for then we can resist the devil and watch him flee (see James 4:7). When our flesh and our own selfish wills are under the leading of the gentle, humble Holy Spirit, then each of us is looking out for the other's best interests and not trying to be in control or win an argument.

It is when we see the whole concept of headship as some form of authoritarian rule, rather than the loving servanthood approach that Jesus intended, that problems occur. Cindy Jacobs explained the consequences of this wrong understanding of headship in her book *Daughters of Destiny*: "The spirit of competition between the husband and wife will be huge because the sin nature of both will want to control the relationship. The sin nature sets up a cycle of judgment as each person in the marriage desires to 'rule' out of selfishness. This is why both submission of the woman to her husband and mutual submission are so very critical in a marriage (see Ephesians 5:21-25). Without both kinds of submission, there is World War III. (Have any of you noticed that?)" [2]

I think her words express the core issue here, that marriage only really works when both husband and wife are functioning in the Spirit and not the flesh nature, and neither is seeking to control the other. I understand that this whole topic is often not as clear-cut as this, and it can be particularly trying when a woman has a husband who is not a believer, is in rebellion, or does not always want to hold up his end of the bargain.

It is critical to state again here that we are never required to submit to our husbands when they ask us to be involved in sin or abuse. In these cases, we must follow Jesus first and even ask for help, if the situation is threatening for us or those around us.

It is often in cases where there is an area of wounding that problems occur. The situation is infected with a seeping wound, and, therefore, things get out of perspective. I have noticed that when I am hurt or out of balance in my relationship with the Lord, I find it much harder to submit my will, as I am afraid and try to fight for myself, rather than yielding and allowing Jesus to help me. It is when we, as women, are in this state that we can fall into control or manipulation in order to push through our own will. This only breeds more disunity, and is in direct opposition to the way of our Lord Jesus. We can be tempted to do this when we are angry, afraid, or just plain selfish, but this is not to be the way of God's warrior wives.

We can be sure of one thing—that we won't get it right all the time. Take Sarah and Abraham, for example. They are two of our great heroes of the faith, but both made some pretty bad blunders in their marriage. Abraham allowed Sarah to be taken away to a pagan king on two occasions (see Genesis 12 and 20) because he was too frightened to admit that she was his wife (imagine having to submit to that idea). We can glean encouragement here from the fact that while Sarah agreed to this plan, God intervened and ensured that neither of the kings laid a hand on her. He protected her, despite the weaknesses of her own husband.

Then, this great example of a submissive wife, Sarah, manipulated her husband into sleeping with her maid, because she couldn't wait for the God-given promise of a child of her own to arrive (see Genesis 16). Here again, God was there to help. He eventually gave Abraham and Sarah a child, not allowing Sarah's unbelief and meddling to steal their inheritance.

It is obvious that men and women alike have a problem, and its name is sin, but Jesus is not only able to forgive but also to transform us. He has not left us alone and wants to help us in every way to become the husbands and wives He planned. I believe that, due to the depth of the wound and subsequent infection between men and women, few, if any of us, fully understand the heart and purpose of God in these marital issues. As reconciliation, forgiveness, and much healing is released from the heavens, we will start to see clearer and embrace our destiny to work together as a warrior team like never before. Then we will cover each other's backs from the deceptive and tempting lies of the "snake" and spur each other on to stay ever obedient to the voice of our God. Married warriors, let us fight for our husbands and not against them.

Warrior Women, Arise!

Chapter 17

THE BATTLE FOR OUR CHILDREN

IF GOD HAS GIVEN YOU THE RESPONSIBILITY FOR someone, to nurture and protect, then this chapter is for you. Godly mothers, it is time for us to rise up and fight for the children God has entrusted to our care.

For far too long the enemy has had his way, ravaging our children, and too many times we have been spiritually blinded as to the real battle at hand. We know the enemy hates families, marriage, and the relationship between children and parents. God is our Father, and He created parenthood and ordained that children should be cared for, loved, and protected by their parents, just as He does things for His children.

A child's relationship with his or her parents lays the foundation for the future and affects the ability to trust God. If you are a mother, you have authority over your child, to pray for, protect, and help him or her. Motherhood is one of the greatest callings a woman can have here on earth. We are created to have life grow within our womb, to give birth, and then to nurture that child. Even if we are unable to have children in the natural, for whatever reason, we all have the calling to bring forth and then nurture life.

Motherhood has been terribly ridiculed and belittled, especially in the Western world, and many times there has been a full-scale frontal attack against this calling. Personally I chose to stay at home with my children when they were small, and that decision threw me into one of the greatest battles I had ever fought. At times, I could literally feel the anger of the hordes of hell and their uproar over my decision. I would hear the enemy whisper, "How dare you stay at home?" "What are you doing with your life?" "Get out and do something worthwhile!"

Whether we are working or stay-at-home moms, the fact remains that motherhood throws us into one of the fiercest battles of all. As mothers, our children belong to us, just as they belong to the Father. The battle is for ownership of them. The enemy comes *"to steal and kill and destroy"* (John 10:10). However dramatic it may sound, the enemy is scheming to own your children. He *"prowls around like a roaring lion looking for someone to devour"* (1 Peter 5:8). His best and most successful strategy to date has been to blind mothers to the fact that there is such a battle going on at all.

When we are ignorant of his schemes, Satan usurps authority over our children. If we don't stand up and fight for them, they can very easily fall prey to the wiles of the enemy, and he is free to take them. Our prayers for our children are the greatest and most effective weapon we have. Prayer is a weapon which the enemy cannot stand against, because it releases the supernatural power and will of the King of the Universe here on earth.

Madame Jeanne Guyon, who lived in France in the 17th century, was a woman renowned for her practice of inner prayer. She wrote in her autobiography, "O my God, if the value of prayer were but known, the great advantage which accrues to the soul from conversing with Thee, and what consequence it is of to salvation, everyone would be assiduous in it. It is a stronghold into which the enemy cannot enter. He may attack it, besiege it, and make a noise about its walls; but while we are faithful and hold our station, he cannot hurt us." [1]

Susanna Wesley, mother of the famed brothers Charles and John Wesley, was also a great prayer warrior. Despite having nineteen children, ten of whom survived to adulthood, and a husband who could not always be relied upon, Susanna managed to educate and bring up her children in an atmosphere of structure and order. She did not allow the dismal circumstances around her to dictate the kind of future her children would have but, rather, turned to prayer as a source of strength and hope. She would find time and space for prayer by sitting in the kitchen and placing an apron over her head, and at such times, her children knew they were not to disturb her. She would also weekly take time with each child, to discuss their spiritual state.

Still today, Susanna Wesley is known as the "mother of Methodism," due to the influence the lives and teachings of her sons Charles and John had on society. There is little doubt that the impact of her prayers helped to birth the destiny of her sons, which, in turn, impacted nations. John Wesley once said of his mother that she had taught him more about Christianity than all the theologians of England.

I believe that as God raises up His army of warrior women, He will also release an anointing over mothers to battle for their children in prayer and, in some cases, even snatch them back from the enemy's hands. Some of you may be at the place of Ziklag, where the enemy has stolen your children from you and has them in captivity:

> *When David and his men came to Ziklag, they found it destroyed by fire and their wives and sons and daughters taken captive. So David and his men wept aloud until they had no strength left to weep.*   1 Samuel 30:3-4

Perhaps your children are in rebellion, are on drugs, or have been otherwise enticed by the world. Like David, you may have wept over it until you had no strength left. If so, may God give you the spirit of David, who did not give way to defeat and hopelessness but rather *"strengthened himself in the LORD"* (1 Samuel 30:6, NKJV). David pursued the enemy right into his own camp to get back what he had lost.

It is easy to fall into hopelessness or unbelief when our children are being attacked, but we need to cry out to God for courage to become like lionesses who boldly encircle their cubs. Let us be the ones doing the prowling, and not the enemy!

In the case of David, he recovered all that had been stolen from him and his men:

Nothing was missing: young or old, boy or girl, plunder
or anything else they had taken. David brought every-
thing back.   1 Samuel 30:19

No matter what has been stolen from you and your children, you can get it back.

As we have seen, Deborah was a warrior, but she was also described as a mother in Israel. We do not know if she had children of her own, but it is evident that she had a heart that sought to protect and nurture the nation of Israel. When she saw that the children of Israel were being threatened by an enemy army, she was not afraid to take up arms and go out to fight for the safety of her people:

Village life in Israel ceased,
  ceased until I, Deborah, arose,
  arose a mother in Israel.   Judges 5:7

May God release such a spirit over us that when we see our children under attack, we cannot just stay home, feeling incapable of doing anything. Instead, may we go out to do battle for them.

I have struggled with how to get these two parts of myself together: on the one hand, a mother involved in the practical day-to-day "stuff" and, on the other hand, a dangerous lioness. This is just who we are in the spiritual and in the natural. We can be gentle as a dove toward our children but shrewd as a snake toward the enemy.

How do we do this practically? There are many ways in which we can pray for and protect our children, and each of us needs to be led by the Holy Spirit:

And pray in the Spirit on all occasions with all kinds of prayers and requests. Ephesians 6:18

When God's warrior Spirit started falling on me, I began going into each of my children's rooms and praying for them while they were at school. I played worship music in there, anointed their rooms with oil, prayed, wept, and danced before the Lord. I held pictures of my children in my hand and cried out to God for His plans to be fulfilled in their lives. I broke the power of the enemy, and declared that they belonged to Jesus. Ask the Holy Spirit to lead you as you pray for your children, and don't give up.

When my children leave for school, I pray protection over them, and then I keep myself on constant spiritual alert for them throughout the day. If I sense that they are in danger, I pray. If I sense that they are hurting, I pray. If I sense that they are sinning, I pray.

I want to make it perfectly clear that this is something that is coming from within. It is not a burden for me to pray for my children. In fact, I find myself compelled to do it.

Do not allow yourself to fall into condemnation if you are not praying. Instead, let the Spirit of God work in you, and call out to your Father for His love, power, and anointing.

When my children were very young, on most days I was so exhausted and overwhelmed that the only prayer I could utter was, "God, get me through this day." But that was enough, and He answered me in my desperation. Motherhood is not something we are supposed to be able to accomplish without the Holy Spirit's help.

I felt like a failure as a mother for many years because I tried in my own strength to be a perfect one, always patient and loving. Instead, I often found myself exhausted, angry, and impatient. I so wanted to love my children just as God loves them, and yet I found myself falling short again and again. I slowly began to realize that trying to do it in my own strength was not working. I cried out to God (and still do) for His help in being a good mother, and that works. Let us be mothers in the strength of the Lord.

I have seen how He has transformed me, giving me patience, when I know it was not humanly possible in the circumstances. I still have my bad days, but I am not the person I was ten years ago, five years ago, or even one year ago. Wherever you happen to find yourself in your motherhood, don't lean on your own understanding. There is so much available to us in God—if we are just willing to let go of our successes and failures and, instead, let Him teach us how to be godly mothers today.

Too long we have allowed the world to dictate to us how a mother should act. Even religious, idealistic stereotypes of motherhood have kept us bound, causing us to compare ourselves with one another and try to meet unrealistic expectations. My husband used to say to me that I looked at all the women around me whom I admired, picked out the area in which each was particularly gifted, put these different parts all together, and then held that up as a picture of how I thought I should be. I had Supermom in front of me, and was striving to be like her. Not surprisingly, I was constantly finding myself falling short of the impossible dream.

For example, I have a friend, a mother of six, whom I respect very much. Many times, when I would go to visit her, I would find her baking bread for her family in the midst of lots of activity around her. It looked like such a wonderful idyllic picture that I quickly convinced myself that a good, loving mother bakes for her family. What I didn't realize was that my friend baked out of grace and gifting. In other words, she knew how to bake, enjoyed doing it, and did not find it to be challenging. I, on the other hand, had very little experience with baking and didn't handle trying to do many things at the same time very well.

You can imagine what happened. There I was with my three children in the kitchen, and we were going to bond with each other through baking. I tried to be as calm and in control as possible, but I was feeling pretty stressed inside about this great task ahead. It ended up with the kitchen a mess, a dough that didn't rise, fighting children, and me in pieces, wondering why I couldn't be a better mother.

Now the question is, was I even supposed to bake? Is that the way God wanted me to show love to my children? I saw something beautiful at my friend's house and tried to make it happen for my family too. When I thought about it, I realized that I loved to cook meals and could do so, no matter what was happening around me, and I could handle it with relative ease and peace. This, then, is God's gift to me and, therefore, my gift to my children. Once I realized that, I stopped baking, cooked them some great meals, and was given a baking machine!

Each one of us is a unique creation of our Father in heaven, and this uniqueness should color our motherhood. Let us stop comparing ourselves with the women around us and, instead, find out who we are designed to be. Learn to get to know and like yourself, and then allow that knowledge to permeate your motherhood. As you relax in your role, your children will sense this, and, consequently, be released in their own giftings.

The same is true for those of you called to be spiritual mothers. You can only teach that which you have learned yourself. Give yourself and those you are serving the freedom to be who God created them to be.

While we are discussing this issue of motherhood, I want to point out that ultimately our children belong to the Lord. He is their Creator and heavenly Father. We have the awesome gift of having them on loan for a few years, and during that time, they are ours to love, cherish, and nurture, but not to control. Eventually we will need to hand them over into the care of God, for He knows the plans He has for them, *"plans to prosper"* and *"not to harm"* them, plans to give them *"a hope and a future"* (Jeremiah 29:11). If we hang onto our children or try to steer their lives too strictly, we can actually aid the enemy and hold them back from their destiny. This is even true of spiritual children the Lord may give us. Our goal ought to be to train them and then release them into their own intimate relationship with the Father.

Many a child's life has been ruined by the ungodly chains their mother has forced around their neck. This, I believe, is one of the greatest battles in motherhood, that of learning to let go when it is time for our children to become adults. This is especially true of boys. We may want to keep them as our sweet little angels forever, but, ultimately, they want to become men who can stand on their own two feet.

Not long ago, my seven-year-old son was particularly angry with me over a period of a few days. I was walking him to school one morning and asked him if he was warm enough, and he blew up at me again. My instinct was to remind him that he had no right to speak to me that way, but I suddenly felt led to ask him if he thought I was treating him like a baby. He immediately softened and answered, "Yes, Mom, you treat me like a baby, but I'm a big boy now." It suddenly dawned on me that the main reason for his anger the past few days had been his feelings of frustration. He wanted to grow up and felt that I was not letting him do it.

I realized that my baby was no longer mine. He wanted to take steps into boyhood, and it was crucial that I let him. He is only seven, so he's not moving out tomorrow, but I can allow him more choice in everyday decisions and give him room to grow. I also see that he identifies himself with his father more and more and, consequently, wants to spend time with him. That's not easy for a mother. After all, he is my youngest, and I have been his world. It hurts to let him go, but I know my love can actually wound him if I keep him as "Mommy's little boy."

John Eldredge put it like this in his book *Wild at Heart*, "This is a very hard time in a mother's life, when the father replaces her as the sun of the boy's universe. It is part of Eve's sorrow, this letting go, this being replaced. Few mothers do it willingly; very few do it well ... . Femininity can never bestow masculinity ... . If a mother will not allow her son to become dangerous, if she does not let the father take him away, she will emasculate him." [2]

Letting go of a child, whether a girl or a boy, is hard for us because of the intensity of a mother's love. We have carried the child inside us for nine months, and then sacrificed years of our time, energy, and sleep for them. We want their best, hate to see them hurting, and desperately want to protect them from harm and suffering.

Mary the mother of Jesus had to walk this hard road. She was entrusted to carry the Child of God in the face of public humiliation. She was willing to give up her reputation, her upcoming marriage, family—her everything—in order to become a mother. She trusted God and carried His Son inside of her. She brought Jesus up, taught Him everything she knew, fed Him, washed Him, loved Him, hugged Him. She had been given a great honor, and she was faithful to the task. However, when Jesus reached adulthood, Mary was faced with a test. Suddenly she had to share her son with others, for He had come into His calling and destiny. Jesus no longer identified Himself with his earthly family but, rather, was looking to His Father in heaven to affirm Him.

We see this come to a crisis point in the story when Mary and Jesus' brothers came to see Jesus while He was ministering and asked to speak to Him. He did not respond to their request but answered with another question:

> *He replied to him, "Who is my mother, and who are my brothers?" Pointing to his disciples, he said, "Here are my mother and my brothers. For whoever does the will of my Father in heaven is my brother and sister and mother."*　　　　　　　　　　Matthew 12:48-50

This must have been an extremely painful experience for Mary, as her son was breaking away from her. But she had to let Him go in order for Him to fulfill the task God had given Him. If she had tried to hold on to Him, even because of genuine love and concern, she could have hindered God's will. God was not abandoning her or belittling the role she had played in Jesus' life. He was, rather, pointing out that her time with Jesus had come to an end. She was now to take a step back and be taught by her own son and Lord.

Although we are not mothers to the Son of God, the principles found here can be helpful and valuable for us. As our children begin to discover and then walk in their God-given destiny, it is vital for us to bless and release them, even when we may feel excluded from this new area of their lives. We continue to pray for them and to be available for them, but it is now on their terms. May God give us the heart of Hannah, who cried out to Him for a child, but also was willing to give him back to the service of the Lord:

> *"I prayed for this child, and the LORD has granted me what I asked of him. So now I give him to the LORD. For his whole life he will be given over to the LORD."*
>
> 1 Samuel 1:27-28

We are living in the last days, and our children may accomplish some of the greatest feats ever seen by mankind. Let us protect them and then release them into the mighty army of the Lord. Just as Abraham was faced with the test of being willing to sacrifice his own son to the Lord, so God calls upon us today to lay our children on the altar of worship, entrusting them to Him.

This is also true for those of us who may have spiritual children. Ultimately, they belong to the Lord, and it would be wise to be sensitive to His leading, as to when our role as an advisor and helper may diminish. Let the plans and will of the Lord prevail—even if it means His taking that child from us. This is painful and heart-wrenching, but we live in serious times.

Perhaps our own children will be called to be martyrs for Jesus, so we cannot love them only with a soulish, human love. Our children are also sons and daughters of the living God, and His eternal purposes and destiny for their lives must be given priority.

Maria Woodworth-Etter lost five of her six children, and their loss brought her great sorrow. However, she was also given wondrous visions of them in heaven, as a comfort to her grieving soul. She describes one vision as follows: "Oh, the glorious sight that met my view can never be expressed by mortal tongue! Heaven is located. It is a real city. Its inhabitants are real and not imaginary. If mothers could see their children as I saw them, in all their shining glory, they would never weep for them, but would leave all and follow Jesus. They would let nothing keep them from following Jesus. They would let nothing keep them from meeting their children in heaven, where they are shining in dazzling beauty around God's throne and are watching to give welcome to the Beautiful City. I never think of my children as being in the grave. Oh, no. The loved form that we laid away in the cold grave is nothing but the casket that contained the jewel which is now shining in the Savior's crown." [3]

We may not have to experience the agony of burying our own children, but still they are the Lord's jewels, whom we must surrender to His loving care, trusting that whatever His plan for them, He will ultimately draw them to Himself in eternal bliss. Mothers, surrender your children to a trustworthy and faithful God, but never surrender them to the wiles of the father of lies. When it comes to our children, whether natural or spiritual, let us resist the enemy in every way, yet submit them to God in all areas.

Warrior Women, Arise!

Chapter 18

THE BATTLE WITH PMS

OVER THE PAST TWO YEARS, WHILE I WAS WRITING this book, I started to notice something. About once each month, situations around me started to feel hopeless, and everyday tasks became mountains I could not seem to climb. I became grumpy and tearful over relatively small issues, started searching the house for sweet things (even resorting to eating up the children's Saturday sweets, at times), and generally felt out of sorts. Amazingly enough, every month I was shocked when my husband reminded me that the reason for my behavior was that I was about to get my period, and that everything would be okay in a few days. (This was obviously a man speaking from experience and years of character building, in dealing with a wife who suffers from PMS.)

I don't know how it is for you. Perhaps you don't suffer at all from hormonal changes, and, if that's the case, I am honestly extremely happy for you. However, perhaps some of you can relate to the frustration and feelings of helplessness a woman can experience, as her body lets her down on a regular, let's say monthly, basis.

Premenstrual syndrome (PMS) is the term given to describe the changes that take place in a woman's body and emotions up to about ten days before her monthly period begins. Some of the common effects of PMS on a woman's behavior are mood swings, irritability, aggressiveness, tearfulness, depression, and exhaustion. The effects on a woman's physical body can include tenderness in the breasts, headaches, stomach pains, water retention, and fatigue. Most women experience some form of discomfort before or during their menstruation, but the extent of it differs greatly among individuals. There is no real medical explanation for these symptoms, except that the changes in hormone levels during the menstrual cycle can trigger such effects.

It seems to me that in the world PMS is an accepted phenomenon and, although there may be numerous jokes told about this condition, there is still some understanding of the fact that many women across the earth become weeping, chocolate-eating, dragons once a month. But what do we, as women of God, who want to have our emotions and bodies submitted to His Spirit, do about this problem? I want nothing more than to serve God and to be His warring princess, and I have, therefore, found it very frustrating and even painful that my hormones go haywire once a month. I want to be able to stand up for Jesus and please Him, even during those nightmare days. If God created us as women, which we know He did, then He must understand us and want to help in all areas of our lives.

That's why I decided to include a chapter on PMS. God created us and our menstrual cycles, and He wants to help and heal us in this matter. I also believe that this can be an area of warfare for us, because the enemy can exploit our weaknesses and use them against us.

There has been very little written about this subject by Christian authors, and I think there is far too much taboo connected with it, because we know, as women of God, that we shouldn't be ruled by our emotions or our stomachs, and therefore a lot of us walk around with guilt and condemnation once a month. I want to share with you here some of the things I have learned in my experiences with PMS. Most of all, it is my desire to let those of you who suffer know that you are not alone, that God cares, and that there is a way to win this battle. We'll look at this whole subject from three different angles: physical, psychological, and spiritual.

THE PHYSICAL ASPECT

Premenstrual syndrome causes physical changes in our bodies, and there are a number of practical things we can do to reduce its effects. Denise Frangipane has given us some good tips in a pamphlet entitled *Deliverance from PMS*. [1]

Cutting down on our intake of sugar, salt, and caffeine days before, and even during, menstruation can lessen the negative effects on the body. Caffeine interferes with the absorption of iron, which reduces our energy levels and also reduces our levels of vitamins B and C. Too much salt can cause an increase in blood pressure and also cause us to retain water. Sugar ... , well, we all know it is not our best friend, but we often crave it. Sugar "messes" with our body chemistry, and this results in tiredness, head-aches, and even irritability, as it causes instability in our blood sugar levels.

Calcium levels in the body will also decrease about a week before our menstruation, and this can also cause tiredness, headaches, and irritability. If we supplement our calcium intake during these days, that can help. Also it is recommended that we take extra B vitamins (in particular B-6), as these vitamins support the nervous system and give the body a boost in han-dling stress. Getting plenty of extra rest and exercising regularly also help to keep us balanced and healthy.

THE PSYCHOLOGICAL ASPECT

Then there is the whole area of how PMS affects us psychologically. I'm sure I don't have to convince you that our emotions and thoughts can get pretty mixed up and out of balance during this time of the month. Perhaps some of you get very weepy or are more prone to anger. I tend to experience both. I am often very emotional just hours before my period comes, and I find myself weeping uncontrollably over issues where perspective and facts may be greatly distorted.

I usually try to turn to Jesus at these times and let the waves of emotion wash over Him. This can be a way for you to channel your emotions without hurting others. Give them to Jesus, and allow them to bring you closer to Him in the midst of the sadness, anger, or depression. He can take it. Our PMS does not frighten Him.

If you struggle with aggression, irritation, and anger during this time, you can even turn these things into something positive. Woman in general, but especially Christian women, are not supposed to have these emotions or qualities. In fact, women who have them are often ostracized or badly judged. However, when you experience them purely because of physical changes in your body, they do not make you a monster. It is what we do with them that is important and determines whether they turn into sinful behavior or not.

What would happen if we turned our emotions toward the enemy, channeling those emotions into warfare for our families, or for our own lives? Submit your emotions to the Holy Spirit and allow yourself to get angry with the enemy. In this way, turn your aggression into prayer, prayer that can set the captives free. I don't know if this is always possible, but why not? Let's not be victims to the changes in our bodies, but, instead, find a way to use these changes to glorify Jesus.

Perhaps you are someone who only gets angry when you have PMS. Well, instead of condemning yourself for that, use it to release the prayer warrior inside of you. If we are going to learn to fight, we need to somehow get activated. We need to allow the Spirit of God to rise up within us and, in Jesus' name, stand against this foul enemy. Frustration will then be turned to victory.

In whatever form you may suffer or be challenged due to your hormones—be it during pregnancy, nursing a baby, going through menopause, or simply having your monthly period—know that God is with you. Try not to take yourself too seriously during these times. Be kind to yourself, have grace, and be sure to separate physical changes in your life from your true spiritual status as a child of God.

Admit that you are in a phase that does not truly represent your character the rest of the month. Try not to make any life-changing decisions, and, especially, don't make any great assessments or conclusions about yourself.

It was actually a good friend of mine who suggested this to me, while I was discussing this topic with her. She helped me to see that it is foolish and even damaging to make assessments about a situation, and especially yourself, when your emotions are out of balance, as one's ability to make objective judgments is seriously hindered.

I experienced it one morning while I was getting my children ready for school. They were teasing each other. I was tired, emotional, and weepy, and after dropping them off at school, I made the wonderfully balanced assessment that the past twelve years of motherhood had been a complete waste of time! (I'm sure that none of you are so immature and emotional as to start analyzing your life so drastically, but, unfortunately once a month I tend to do it.) I remember thinking about what my friend had said, and I was able to stop myself, turning away from my self-pity and negativity toward God and His perspective.

THE SPIRITUAL ASPECT

This is where the spiritual battle enters the picture, affording us the opportunity to use the spiritual weapons we have been given:

> *We demolish arguments and every pretension that sets itself up against the knowledge of God, and we take captive every thought to make it obedient to Christ.*
>
> 2 Corinthians 10:5

We do not need to accept the negative thoughts that come to us during PMS. The Holy Spirit wants to help us to learn to fight in this area, no longer seeing ourselves as victims, but as victors. We can capture negative thoughts and make them our prisoners, rather than becoming their slaves. I know this is not easy, and if you have PMS right now, you may be tempted to throw this book at the wall. But it is true; we can control our thought life with the help of a loving God, and we can live a victorious life, even when we suffer from PMS.

This is where the battle rages, in our thought life, which the enemy wants to infiltrate in order to hurt us at this vulnerable time. Denise Frangipane addressed this in her pamphlet. She wrote: "Satan's strategy is to come at us when we are most vulnerable. He takes advantage of women who are prone toward hormonal imbalances during this time of the month. If he can make us think there is no way out, that our problems are purely physical, then he can defeat us."

She continued: "Of course hormonal problems are physical, but Satan often uses our physical circumstances to mask his activities. The strength of Satan's lie is in its disguise and how successfully he can blend it into our thinking." [2]

I am sure many of you have felt powerless, condemned, and a failure when you have found yourself saying or doing things out of character, while experiencing PMS. The enemy throws his accusations and lies at us, and we become crushed under the weight of condemnation. At these times, we can turn to our Father in repentance, ask others for forgiveness (when necessary), resist the enemy, and allow God to put us back on our feet again.

When Paul wrote about taking every thought captive, he was actually giving practical guidelines for the believer's warfare in this world:

For though we live in the world, we do not wage war as the world does. The weapons we fight with are not the weapons of the world. On the contrary, they have divine power to demolish strongholds. 2 Corinthians 10:3-4

One of our greatest weapons during bouts of PMS, and any other time that negative thoughts bombard us, is to refuse to engage them. This is something we can train in. Just as when you start to do bodybuilding, your muscles may hurt at first, because they're not accustomed to being used, but gradually they become stronger and are able to withstand greater pressure.

We can do our part to lessen the effects of PMS, but the best news for us is this: As with any area in which we may struggle as women, we have a God who is totally committed to helping and delivering us. The past few months I have spent a considerable amount of time in the presence of God, not trying to perform, not fighting the enemy, not asking for help with my PMS, but just receiving His love, and I have noticed that the negative symptoms related to PMS have been reduced significantly. Let's saturate ourselves with God, who is the Creator of all life, and experience how He transforms our bodies and souls, without human striving.

As women, let us learn to accept our bodies, to laugh, and, above all, to show love and grace to ourselves. Premenstrual syndrome does not disqualify you from being a warrior. In fact, it is something you can become the victor over and even turn against the enemy.

Warrior Women, Arise!

Chapter 19

THE BATTLE WITH THE TONGUE

DR. LILLIAN YEOMANS WAS A WOMAN WHO WAS set free by the power of Jesus after years of addiction to drugs, and, subsequently, gave up her profession as a doctor and traveled extensively, teaching and preaching on the healing power of God. In May of 1926 she wrote the following: "When I was a child I was filled with misgivings each time my mother lined me up in front of a doctor, for the first thing he said to me was, 'Put out your tongue!' And when I put out my poor, little trembling tongue, he would make an awful frown, 'This child has been eating trash. Give her no supper and put her early to bed.' Worse, he would say, 'Give her a dose of castor oil!' I used to think, How wise he must be! How can he possibly tell what's wrong with me just by looking at my tongue?

"When I got older and became a doctor myself, I would say to my patients, 'Put out your tongue!' I had learned that a clean pink tongue was the very index of health; and that a swollen, discolored furry tongue was a sure indication that something was seriously wrong.

"Then I found the Great Physician and commenced to study His Book. My expansive medical library was reduced to just one volume. In it, I found a remedy for every ailment, spiritual and physical, to which flesh is heir. When we say yes to Jesus, we must put out our tongues—examine ourselves to see what it is that is in our hearts, for it shall surely come to our tongues." [1]

The book of James deals with the issue of the human tongue. It is such a small part of our body, but when used unwisely, it can cause great damage:

Likewise the tongue is a small part of the body, but it makes great boasts. Consider what a great forest is set on fire by a small spark. The tongue also is a fire, a world of evil among the parts of the body.   James 3:5-6

Every person has had to contend with the power of the tongue, trying to gain control over it, and very few have succeeded. What comes out of our mouths comes from the overflow of our hearts. If there is any anger, hatred, bitterness, revenge, malice, or unkindness there, it will be exposed. Often in stressful situations these hidden attitudes are unveiled. If we are to be success-ful warrior women in our battle against sin and evil, we must allow the Spirit of God to have more control over our hearts and, consequently, over our tongues.

Let's face it; most women love to talk. We love to discuss situations and, especially, people around us. We love to express our emotions, thoughts, longings, and fears. Many of us are verbal processors, and talking helps us evaluate our lives. This, in itself, is not sinful or wrong. It can be part of who God has created us to be.

However, women can also be some of the worst gossips and slanderers. We can spread rumors and false accusations and be used by the enemy to wound and, in some cases, destroy other people. We can work together with the spirits of accusation and criticism and leave poison and destruction in our wake.

We can even do this unintentionally, by simply agreeing with the accusations of the enemy. If we are to arise as an army of warrior women, God will need to take us to a higher level of integrity and purity in our lives in this regard:

Do not let any unwholesome talk come out of your mouths, but only what is helpful for building others up according to their needs, that it benefit those who listen. And do not grieve the Holy Spirit of God, with whom you were sealed for the day of redemption. Get rid of all bitterness, rage and anger, brawling and slander, along with every form of malice. Ephesians 4:29-31

The Holy Spirit is grieved when we speak in a way that hurts each other and, consequently, may cause Him to withdraw His presence. I know that when my children fight or speak unkindly to one another, it hurts me deeply. How much more must the Holy Spirit grieve, when He sees God's own children wounding each other with careless and hurtful words.

I don't know about you, but I desperately want the presence of the Holy Spirt in my life, and I never want to cause Him to withdraw from me, even for a moment.

This requires discipline and an awareness of what we say, but discipline alone does not always deal with the fruits of our tongue. We must get to the root of the matter.

If you know that you are a gossip, you can make a decision to stop, which is good, but you can also allow God to show you where this stronghold came into your life. Perhaps your mother was a gossip, or you learned this behavior from your friends at school. Is there jealousy, insecurity, or pride in your life, that causes you to speak badly about others?

In your communication with others, is there anger, frustration, irritation, control, or put-downs in your speech? When you are under pressure at work, at home, or in the car, what comes out of your mouth? God does not want to condemn us in this. He knows what is in our hearts, even before we do. He sees everything, and it does not affect His undying love for us. He is committed to us, no matter what we say or do. However, He does want to transform us to be like Him, not only in our actions, but also in our speech. In Jesus, there is no malice, gossip, or unkind words. If, then, we are to fully represent Him to the world, these tendencies have to go.

Words have power, and God created the world by the power of His words. He simply spoke, and things came into being. If we are created in His image, then our words also have the ability to create life. God takes this aspect of our lives so seriously that He stated through Jesus:

"I tell you that men will have to give account on the day of judgment for every careless word they have spoken. For by your words you will be acquitted, and by your words you will be condemned." Matthew 12:36-37

We do not need to live in a destructive fear that God is out to condemn us every day. Instead, let us live in the healthy fear of the Lord.

The fear of the Lord reminds us that God is King and that one day we will meet Him face to face and give account for the way in which we have lived our lives here on earth. God wants us to be His success stories. He has given us the Holy Spirit to enable us to find wisdom and strength in every situation. He also knows our weaknesses and remembers that we are but dust. Here again, it is a matter of the heart. We may not be perfect in what we say, but if our heart attitude is that we want to change, want to talk like Jesus, then we are on the right track.

If we "blow it," we don't need to stay in defeat. Rather, we should run boldly to God, asking for His forgiveness. If we have hurt others with our words, we can humbly ask them for forgiveness as well. This is hard, but it is not impossible. If you see that your tongue is an area of weakness in your life (which, if we're honest, it is for most of us), ask God for help.

Don't focus on what you shouldn't say, but focus on what He says about you. Despite our inadequacies, He is full of faith and hope toward us. Jesus is interceding for us day and night and stands between us and the Father, allowing us to be totally acceptable (see Romans 8:34).

The more we receive this incredible, unconditional love in our lives, the more we will see and treat others accordingly. As our hearts are filled with grace, so our tongues will be filled with the same, speaking kind and gentle words toward others.

This is not a battle we can fight by our own willpower or positive thinking. Let the fire of God be released in your life. Cry out to Him for purification, as Isaiah did. He realized that he was a man with an unclean mouth, and God sent an angel with coals of fire from heaven to purify his lips (see Isaiah 6:5-6). This is a process and a work of grace, but let's choose to work with God on it.

The enemy allies himself with our sinful nature, to cause us to speak out binding and hurtful words over others and ourselves. In my own life, this has been a great stronghold. Whenever hopelessness and unbelief would flow over me, I would speak out negative statements such as, "There's no use," "I can't cope with this," and "I'll never be able to become what God wants me to be." In these situations I allowed my emotions to rule, and I placed myself in even greater bondage by agreeing with the enemy.

Words spoken over us as children, especially by those who had authority over us—parents and teachers for example—can follow us later in life. For example, a child told that he or she will never amount to much will, at some point, begin to believe it, and it becomes a self-fulfilling curse in their lives. If you are aware of any of these statements that affect you today, find someone you trust to pray with you and break the power of those words. Allow

God to show you what words He speaks over your life, and look at all the promises and declarations of love He has already spoken over you through His Living Word.

If God is going to use us as mighty warriors, proclaiming His Word to others, He must be able to trust us. Let's get free from all exaggeration, cynicism, pride, lying, and malice. Pray that the stream coming out of your mouth will be pure and full of life.

It is also crucial that we be aware that our battle is not just with the evil thoughts within us, but that the enemy works from the outside also. There are evil spirits of accusation, criticism, and gossip which try to infiltrate ministries, churches, families, and organizations. They gain access by placing thoughts in the minds of the people, to accuse, judge, or criticize those around them. If we submit to these thoughts and then start to express them, the enemy has gained ground.

These accusations are often directed toward leaders of a certain group. The enemy knows that a camp divided against itself *"cannot stand"* (Mark 3:24-25); therefore, he seeks to bring division and mistrust. Such accusations may start as small words, but, like yeast, they will grow and eventually work through the whole lump of dough.

Jesus warned His disciples:

"Be careful. ... Be on your guard against the yeast of the Pharisees and Sadducees."   Matthew 16:6

The Pharisees were full of self-righteousness and judgment. Whenever we are tempted to judge or accuse, let us fling ourselves on the mercy of the Lord and cry out for the cloak of humility. Never receive an accusation about another person without checking it out first. Then, if it is true, call out to God for that person. We know that the enemy accuses us day and night before the throne of God, but Jesus intercedes for us, instead, and His love covers all accusations.

If you see weakness or even sin in another person's life, turn to intercession for that person. Call out to God for His grace for them. If it is a serious sin, of course, we should address it, either by approaching the person in love and/or going to someone in leadership who has the maturity to handle it. But, whatever we do, we cannot take on the attitude of the enemy and hope to help that person.

Jesus sees each one of us and our weaknesses, but how does He deal with us? It is His kindness that leads us to repentance. When He convicts, there is never accusation, but truth, spoken in love, that brings hope and conviction. When you feel yourself tempted with thoughts of accusation do what James taught:

> *Submit yourselves, then, to God. Resist the devil, and he will flee from you.* James 4:7

As warriors, we must be aware of the enemy's tactics and refuse to submit to his plans. Rise up as a warrior of God, and use your tongue as a weapon to bring blessing, truth, and life into the darkness around you.

Warrior Women, Arise!

Chapter 20

THE WARRIOR AT THE CROSS

THE LORD IS CALLING US TO RISE UP AND TAKE our place in His army, but this is a decision that cannot be made lightly, as it involves surrendering one's time, dreams, will, relationships, and, very possibly, even one's own life. In times of war, those who enlist do so in the knowledge that their lives will no longer be their own. Even if they should survive the war, their decision to serve will surely affect them for many years to come.

When they enlist, they must say goodbye to family, friends, home and career and enter into boot camp for a time. There, the first thing they experience is to have their hair cut short, next they are given military clothing, and then a time of rigorous training and discipline begins.

The new recruits are taught to submit to and trust their commanding officers. This is often an excruciating time, as their old self is slowly burned away in the fire of discipline. This time, which can appear as merciless and cruel, is fundamentally crucial, in order to transform a group of willful individuals into a skilled, obedient, and fully-equipped army. Each soldier is no longer focused on his or her individual desires, but is committed to a greater cause. In fact, it is often this hard training that saves these soldiers' lives when they are faced with the frightful realities of war. Without their boot camp experience and training, sending them out to war would be a suicide mission.

The same principles apply for us, women of God. If God is calling us to sign up in His army, then we should weigh this invitation carefully. If we do sign up, the Lord is asking us to surrender our wills, our everything, in order to follow Him. This is the basic invitation of the cross:

"If anyone would come after me, he must deny himself and take up his cross and follow me. For whoever wants to save his life will lose it, but whoever loses his life for me will find it." Matthew 16:24-25

Jesus invites us into a life of eternity and oneness with Him, where we lay ourselves on His altar and offer ourselves as living sacrifices. Yet, when He calls us, it is not as a cold, demanding army officer, but as Friend and Lover of our souls. Jesus asks us for everything because He wants to replace our "ME" with His great "I AM." He offers us everything, yet it is impossible to receive from Him if we are not willing to surrender.

It is the Lord's kindness that asks us to yield our own wills before He leads us into battle, because He knows that only an obedient child, one who understands the orders of his or her commanding officer, is safe in a war situation. The King of Kings knows all things, including what is best for us. Therefore, it is vital for us to trust Him.

In an earlier chapter I mentioned Madame Jeanne Guyon of France and the fact that she was renowned for her practice of inner prayer. What I didn't say there was that she was severely persecuted for her writings and practices, even being imprisoned on numerous occasions. While reading her autobiography, I was deeply touched by her attitude toward the cross and the repeated sufferings she experienced.

As a child, she was beaten and falsely accused of wrongdoing, and then, as an adult, these persecutions and injustices intensified and even followed her to her grave. She was persecuted for her practice of seeking God through inner prayer, rather than through outward penance, a revolutionary idea in Catholic France at that time. Her teachings of totally releasing one's life to God and allowing oneself to be led by His Holy Spirit were also a threat to the established church. However, she saw all her sufferings as gifts from the Lord and not punishments.

Jeanne Guyon gladly embraced the crosses in her life, seeing how they were used to transform her into God's likeness. Even in times of great suffering and pain, she experienced a supernatural peace and joy. She discovered a secret, which, I believe, is sadly lost to much of the church today, namely that of the joy, honor, and necessity of embracing the cross as a follower of Jesus.

To give you an insight into her life, I quote from the last page of her autobiography, written in prison around 1700. She wrote: "While I was a prisoner in Vincennes, and Monsieur de La Reine examined me, I passed my time in great peace, content to pass the rest of my life there, if such were the will of God. I sang songs of joy, which the maid who served me learned by heart, as fast as I made them. We together sang thy praises, O, my God! The stones of my prison looked in my eyes like rubies; I esteemed them more than all the gaudy brilliancies of a vain world. My heart was full of that joy which Thou givest to them who love thee, in the midst of their greatest crosses.

"When things were carried to the greatest extremities, being then in the Bastille, I said, 'O, my God, if You are pleased to render me a new spectacle to men and angels, Thy holy will be done!' " [1]

This attitude toward suffering is probably foreign to many of us, and I must confess that it is not always easy for me to truly thank God for my pains. In an age when the church often runs from every form of hardship, and especially suffering, we have something to learn from this warrior woman of the past. For most people in the Western world, it does not cost that much to take the first step toward following Jesus. They may be laughed at or scorned by some relatives or others in society, but, generally, their decision can go largely unnoticed and uncontested. However, for many millions of people in this same world, the decision to become a Christian involves embracing the cross immediately.

For example, in the Muslim world, for one to convert to Christianity can involve immediate death or expulsion from family and society. Those who choose to follow Jesus are faced with the reality that their decision means dying to self, in many cases, literally. At the same time, they often experience overwhelming love from Jesus. The peace and joy of finally knowing the God they have searched for all their lives empowers them to freely accept persecution, rather than live without the Savior. The message of the cross needs to be revived and preached in Western Christianity again, not to condemn, but, rather, to liberate us from the love of self, perhaps our most deadly enemy.

Madame Guyon did not try to change in her own strength, nor was her character developed overnight. In order to come to the place where she could write the above words, she had been trained and tried in the fires of God. As with all of us, her understanding of the cross developed through a process, during which she experienced many failures and times of extreme darkness and hopelessness, as well as unspeakable expressions of God's passionate love for her. Yet, the treasures she learned about the power of inner prayer with her God and enduring the cross shook a whole nation.

Too often we consider suffering as something negative to be avoided at all costs, but I pray the Lord will give us revelation and wisdom in this time to see that it can become our greatest ally:

Let us fix our eyes on Jesus, the author and perfecter of our faith, who for the joy set before him endured the cross, scorning its shame, and sat down at the right hand of the throne of God. Hebrews 12:2

Jesus was able to endure all that He suffered because of the joy He knew awaited Him after His trials. When we truly understand the love of the Father for us and what awaits us in Paradise, this will give us the ability to endure all the hardships we may face here on earth.

Persecution has nothing to do with God's love for us. It is just an inevitable consequence of being a true follower of Jesus. He taught that no servant is greater than his master and that if the world hated Him, so it would also hate and persecute us (see John 15:18-21). If we are to fight and be victorious in these last-day battles, this lost treasure must be rediscovered and embraced by the church of Christ.

The enemy sent all kinds of attacks against Madame Guyon, to quench her love and to steal this discovery, but she was able to stand victorious, no matter her outward circumstances. Her inner peace and joy were not dependent upon the external, and, therefore, the enemy could not touch her. This is a secret that could best be learned by all of us in these times. If we have surrendered all to Jesus, then there is nothing the enemy can take from us, not even life itself.

I must confess that in writing this I am deeply convicted and shaken in my own life. I love Jesus and want to give Him everything, yet the thought of the unknown and future persecutions can shake me at times. I see that I am not made complete in love yet, and all I can do is cry out to God to fill me with more of His love. We know that perfect love casts out fear (see 1 John 4:18), and, therefore, the more we allow God's love to saturate our hearts and minds, the less we will fear.

Don't let the enemy accuse you in all this talk about the cross. Condemnation, fear, unbelief, and doubt never come from the Father. Instead, walk with me into the Holy Spirit's conviction, as He helps and comforts us, giving us all the strength we need to follow Him to the end.

I believe that very few, if any, of God's people are totally ready or equipped for what is coming, yet I know that our Lord is faithful, and for Him one day is as a thousand years (see 2 Peter 3:8). If we give Him the little we have today, surrendering to the degree we are able, He can work with that and begin to transform and prepare us. Just as there is no one righteous (see Romans 3:12), there is no one who can serve God in his or her own strength. It is by grace that we are saved, and it is grace that will lead us on.

Jesus is returning for a pure and spotless bride. Our part is to yield; His is to transform and purify us. The King of Kings is inviting us into the battle of the ages for the souls of men. Let us choose to freely submit our wills in His boot camp, so that He may transform us into a powerful army of warrior women.

Warrior Women, Arise!

Chapter 21

THE CONCLUSION

THE FATHER HAS PLANNED SOMETHING FOR HIS daughters, and I believe He wants to remind us today:

"I am God, and there is no other;
  I am God and there is none like me.
I make known the end from the beginning,
  from ancient times, what is still to come.
I say: My purpose will stand,
  and I will do all that I please. ...
What I have said, that will I bring about;
  what I have planned, that will I do."

Isaiah 46:9-11

He is God, and He can fix this thing. If we look at our own lives and at most of those around us, to become fearsome warriors will require a miracle. Our part in this is to surrender ourselves to our God and allow Him to love, equip, and release us.

I have talked to and prayed with many women while writing this book, and almost all of them are fighting their own battles and need Jesus to come through for them as their Victor. Few feel as if they are mighty warriors right now, but most have a longing to become one. It seems that God's women are like the many dry bones in the valley that Ezekiel saw so many years ago. He was asked by the Lord:

"Son of man, can these bones live?" Ezekiel 37:3

It's a question we may ask ourselves today. Ezekiel wisely answered:

"O Sovereign Lord, you alone know." (same verse)

The situation in Ezekiel's day looked hopeless and helpless, just as it may appear at present. Yet, I believe the words of the Lord given to Ezekiel are resounding and prophesying over the women of God today:

"Dry bones, hear the word of the Lord! This is what the Sovereign Lord says to these bones: I will make breath enter you, and you will come to life. I will attach tendons to you and make flesh come upon you and cover you with skin; I will put breath in you, and you will come to life." Ezekiel 37:4-6

Soon there will be the sound of rattling across the world, as the bones come together, and flesh and tendons appear. Then the breath from the four winds will come and breathe into the slain women of God, and we will come to life and stand on our feet—*"a vast army"* (Ezekiel 37:10).

Warrior Women, Arise!

ENDNOTES

Chapter 1:
1. Willard Trask (translator and compiler) and Sir Edward S. Creasy (the afterword), *Joan of Arc, in Her Own Words* (New York: Turtle Point Press, 1996), 37.
2. Ibid, 19.
3. Ibid, 144.
4. Ibid, 144.
5. Ibid, 12.
6. Ed Silvoso, *Women: God's Secret Weapon* (Ventura, California: Gospel Light, 2001), 17.
7. Cindy Jacobs, *Women of Destiny* (Ventura, California: Gospel Light, 1998), 282.

Chapter 2:
1. Willard Trask (translator and compiler) and Sir Edward S. Creasy (the afterword), *Joan of Arc, in Her Own Words,* 41.

Chapter 3:
1. JW. Martin, (compiler), *The Spirit-Filled Woman* (Lake Mary, Florida: Creation House, 1997), 28.
2. Miep Gies, from an article in the January 13, 2010 edition of *Breaking Christian News.* Written by Teresa Neumann, the article was entitled: "Miep Gies, Who Helped Hide Anne Frank, Dies at Age 100."
3. Anne Frank, *The Diary of a Young Woman, The Definitive Edition* (New York: The Penguin Group, 2007), 250.

Chapter 4:
1. Sun Tzu, *The Art of War, Limited Edition,* English translation by Lionel Giles (El Paso, Texas: El Paso Norte Press, 2005), 13.
2. Ed Silvoso, *Women: God's Secret Weapon,* 16.
3. Ibid, 17.

Chapter 5:
1. Benny Hinn, *The Anointing* (Milton Keynes, England: Word Publishing, 1992), 78, 79.

Chapter 6:
1. Ed Silvoso, *Women: God's Secret Weapon,* 46.
2. Corrie Ten Boom, with John and Elizabeth Sherrill, *The Hiding Place* (London, England: Hodder and Stoughton, 1971), 220, 221.
3. Lewis B. Smedes, *The Art of Forgiving* (New York: Ballantine Books, 1996), 178.

Chapter 8:
1. You can view this clip at http://www.youtube.com/watch?v=7rSjh52fGTg.
2. You can view this clip at http://www.dove.ca/facilitators/#/features/videos/video_gallery.aspx[cp-documentid=9150778]/.

Chapter 9:
1. JW. Martin (compiler), *The Spirit-Filled Woman*, 191.
2. From a film clip of Kathryn Kuhlman speaking to a large audience in 1975 posted to YouTube on December 26, 2006.

Chapter 10:
1. Maria Woodworth-Etter, *Signs and Wonders* (New Kensington, Pennsylvania: Whitaker House Publishers, 1997), 15.

Chapter 13:
1. Maria Woodworth-Etter, *Signs and Wonders,* 18.
2. Ibid, 16.
3. Ibid, 16.
4. Ibid, 22.

Chapter 14:
1. JW. Martin (compiler), *The Spirit-Filled Woman,* 115.
2. John Vance Cheney, from his poem "Tears," *The Century*, Vol. 44, Issue 4 (August 1892).
3. Taken from an article entitled "A Key to Breakthrough in 2010: A Broken and Contrite Heart," by Paul Keith Davis, placed on The Elijah List website December 12, 2009.
4. Gwen Shaw, from an article taken from *End-Time Handmaidens & Servants Magazine* No. 64, October, 2004, 21-22. The article was entitled "Teach Them to Weep!"

Chapter 15:
1. Al Hsu, *The Single Issue* (Leicester, England: Inter-Varsity Press, 1997), 62.
2. Ibid, 184.
3. Ibid, 184.

4. http://www.sidroth.org/site/PageServer?pagename=tv_archives_2009.

5. Faith Cook, *Seeing the Invisible: Ordinary People of Extraordinary Faith* (Durham, England: Evangelical Press, 1998), 104.

6. Ibid, 105.

7. Ibid, 114.

Chapter 16:

1. According to Jewish law at that time, when a couple became betrothed, they were deemed legally married from that point on. This would explain why the Bible states that Joseph was thinking to divorce Mary, even though there had been no wedding ceremony.

2. Cindy Jacobs, *Women of Destiny* (Ventura, California: Gospel Light, 1998), 211.

Chapter 17:

1. Jeanne Guyon, *The Autobiography of Madame Guyon* (Sioux Falls, South Dakota: Nu Vision Publications, LLC, 2007), 26.

2. John Eldredge, *Wild at Heart* (Nashville, Tennessee: Thomas Nelson, Inc., 2001), 64.

3. Maria Woodworth-Etter, *Signs and Wonders,* 15.

Chapter 18:

1. Denise Frangipane, *Deliverance from PMS* (Bethesda, Maryland: Arrow Publications, 1992).

2. Ibid, 13.

Chapter 19:

1. JW. Martin (compiler), *The Spirit-Filled Woman,* 34.

Chapter 20:

1. Jeanne Guyon, *The Autobiography of Madame Guyon,* 209.

For more information about this book or to contact the author, go to: www.warriorwomenarise.com

CPSIA information can be obtained
at www.ICGtesting.com
Printed in the USA
LVHW090403030419

612789LV00001B/18/P